IN DRAKE'S WAI

The Early Voyages

Francis Drake becomes rich and gains influence

1566-1577

Michael Turner

The first pictorial and topographical Drake biography. The only biography to describe every landfall, anchorage and to retrace fully, Drakes footsteps in England and abroad.

Dedicated with the pinnacle of gratitude to the late
Mr Raymond Aker,
President of The Drake Navigators Guild,
Palo Alto, California

First published in 2005

Published by
Paul Mould Publishing UK

in association with
Empire Publishing Services USA

Library of Congress C-I-P data can be obtained from
the British Library, Boston Spa

ISBN 1-904959-21-0

Printed in Great Britain by
CLE Print Limited

CONTENTS

PHOTOGRAPHS

MAPS

INTRODUCTION

The Author

Michael Turner is a secondary school teacher of physical
education and humanities. Concurrent with his research on
Drake, Michael has studied Spanish, which has been the most
useful language during his travels. He is usually the sole field
worker. Michael began backpacking through seventy countries
aged 20. He soon developed a passion for photo-journalism. He
published narrated slide packs on human rights. This interest
gained him audiences with Mother Teresa and Nelson Mandela.
Illustrated travel features appeared in travel and photographic
magazines. In 1980 Michael noticed Drake's portrait in a
Mexican fortress. This inspired him to photograph all the
places in the world Drake visited. Illustrated Drake articles
appeared in books, magazines and newspapers. This lead to
appearing on local television news features in England and
Chile. On a national level, Michael was interviewed on several
BBC radio programmes. In 1996 Michael co-presented a BBC2
documentary to mark the 400th anniversary of Drake's death
and was interviewed in Spanish for a similar programme in
Panamá. In 2001 Michael contributed towards a Sky History
documentary on Drake's world voyage. As usual, his pictures
were used. Michael has lectured to the illustrious Royal
Geographical Society and to Britain's largest lecturing group
the Ashridge Circle. Michael has received a Rolex Award For
Enterprise. Michael's *In Drake's Wake* project appears on the
Internet along with the *Drake Exploration Society* which he
founded.

Preface

Over 250 biographies have been written about Sir Francis Drake but this one is unique. Authors have usually manifested their poetic and literary prowess by interpreting the contemporary documents into modern-day prose. Some writers have simply re-written other authors' works and their mistakes. This archival and armchair approach has naturally perpetuated the errors and often side-stepped any vague topographical descriptions found in the primary narratives. These can only be solved by field studies. It took twenty years to write this book, hence the text is the most accurate and topographically detailed. One advantage of "seeing" and "touching" Drake's life in this way is that the reader can appreciate the context of geography and 16th century dimensions of settlements, against which Drake's raiding activities can be assessed. This book examines Drake's achievements and failings objectively without excessive hero worship. Most significantly, this is the only biography to describe every Drake landfall, anchorage and to retrace fully, his footsteps in England and abroad, no matter how brief or insignificant. The illustrated topographically biased text uniquely lends itself to recount numerous Drake events, which have been omitted from the conventional biography.

All definitely identified places appear in bold type. A place that Drake might have visited, or is related to the Drake story is underlined. To avoid confusion, where round brackets have been used by the authors of the contemporary texts, I have used square brackets.

This book has been written mainly from the primary sources, most of which were compiled during Drake's voyages. I have resorted to quoting the narratives when they refer to the topography that can be photographed. To highlight their authenticity and enhance the pictures of the unchanged sites the original spelling has been retained, unless the secondary author has modernised the text. It is hoped that the copious illustrations will make the original narratives more interesting. Where it is linguistically appropriate, I have respected the country's spelling of its place names. The same applies to people's names. To assist the reader in correct pronunciation, accents denote a stress on that syllable. In Spanish they are used to indicate that the stress falls contrary to the grammatical rule.

To give a balanced account, the Spanish versions are also presented. These often harmonise, elaborate or, sometimes contradict the English versions. In some instances, the Spanish contributions are the only sources. If the accounts of an episode are basically repetitive, then the most detailed version is supplied. When Drake visited a location more than once, the pertaining topographical material is not repeated for a subsequent visit. If the write-up for a sojourn is brief, it is because the volume of narration is scant, or has been saved to detail a more eventful visit, for which the accounts are more detailed. To give a sense of time, I have periodically quoted dates from the logs. These can vary a day or two from each other, which I usually consider to be insignificant. The dates used in this book are quoted from the old Julian calendar and the present-day Gregorian calendars. The Julian calendar was ten days earlier than the Gregorian calendar. The latter had been introduced by Pope Gregory XIII and adopted by most of Catholic Europe in 1582. England continued to use the old

Julian, with its year beginning on Lady Day 25 March until September 1752.

For background reasons, I have touched upon Tudor politics and voyage preparations. The standard Drake biographies will guide the reader through this area in greater depth. The main titles of the secondary sources are listed in the bibliography.

To appeal to a wider readership, which includes those who enjoy travelogues, I have discreetly and sparingly inserted my own research techniques and adventures in the field. This humanistic element describes how a site was identified and reached, and should satisfy the inquisitive reader.

I must mention that, if it were not for the patient and distinguished academics, my unique project of putting pictures to Drake's life would not have reached a definitive level. This is because the span of my lifetime would be insufficient for the necessary number of decades of archival research, followed by twenty years of arduous travel. Therefore I see my work as taking over where the academics have left off. This in turn has created a partnership between a century of academic studies and the subsequent field studies. Sir Julian Corbett, the great Victorian naval historian, produced the first classic Drake biography. This ignited subsequent academics to expand upon his work and to publish the sources from which he wrote. My project will be realised a century after Corbett's biographical masterpiece. This will end the most intense century of Drake study.

Project Methodology

All the primary sources for each Drake voyage were meticulously studied and every topographical description was photographed. This enabled me to assume the position from which topographical description was given in the narratives. This brings to life the sparsely illustrated texts, which are characteristic of early modern history.

The size of the area chosen for each expedition depended upon the length of my school holiday. When possible, I visited a region at the same time of year as Drake, thereby optimising the chance of experiencing similar weather and recording the exact vegetation as the chroniclers described. Also, the level of water in the streams would be similar to when Drake watered.

To gain people's confidence, overcome any language barrier and clarify the reason for boat hire a letter from the British embassy in the host country, or from the host country's embassy in London, was invaluable. This was augmented by a growing collection of illustrated published articles in newspapers, books and magazines.

In 1998 I proof-read the near completed manuscript. In the quest for photographic coverage, I decided to re-visit those places where boat hire had been neglected during the 1980s. From 1997 I was able to pinpoint Drake's theoretical distances by using GPS. This navigation device further encouraged the 1998 re-visits. For example, I could measure how far Drake was from Nombre de Dios when he robbed the mule train.

Consequently, one of this book's main strengths is knowing where Drake is at any given point. Finding these "lost anchorages" has constituted many discoveries. I define a "discovery" as not just realising what the site looks like today but:

(i)   having to find the location because its name has changed, or the original site has been abandoned, or has vanished and its whereabouts has baffled authors.

(ii)   amplifying vague descriptions - for example, finding the actual cove in the gulf.

(iii) correcting the contemporary accounts regarding distances and what was supposedly seen.

Acknowledgements

In 1982, the late *James Barber*, then Curator of the Plymouth Museum and Art Gallery, gave me my first valuable academic guidance. Mr Barber kindly drove me to Drake sites in and around Plymouth.

James put me in contact with retired Master Merchant Mariner, *Raymond Aker*, President of the Drake Navigators Guild, Palo Alto, California. Since 1950 Mr Aker had always been a principal participant and with other guild members found the site of Drake's encampment and careening place at Drake's Bay California. The Guild investigated Drake's navigation into the North Pacific and located Drake's landfall and anchorage on the Oregon coast. Mr Aker's studies have also included reconstructing Drake's entire world voyage. From 1983, based upon the mind-set of a navigator, Mr Aker has been my guiding beacon. He has pinpointed many of Drake's "lost anchorages" on all his voyages, corrected and amplified my sleuthing and has substantiated the field discoveries. This, coupled with his charts and sailing directions, have enabled me to embark upon each expedition with maximum information at my disposal. Ray technically moulded all the nautical sections in this book.

Ray gave me the Louisiana address of *Dean Edwin Webster*. Edwin had lived in Panamá and had conducted Drake archaeology, which produced significant finds. Edwin's essays and letters to myself help solve many Drake mysteries.

In 1991 the Panamanian Tourist Bureau introduced me to Sr. *René Gómez* proprietor of Scubapanamá. This diving school also specialised in light salvage work. René always provided valuable and kind logistical support, such as boats and vehicles during the expeditions to Panamá.

In 1991 after receiving national press coverage for my interest in locating Drake's lead casket, I was contacted by history teacher, *Susan Jackson*. I soon discovered that Susan was the world's most read Drake scholar, with 556 books to her credit. The weight of these books meant that her upstairs bedroom floor had to be reinforced! With the mentality of a true historian, she was nothing short of a walking Drake encyclopaedia. Her knowledge on Elizabethan England was second to none. Therefore I am eternally grateful for her enormous contribution towards the Drake in England sections. No recorded or perceived Drake location has been omitted due to her meticulous archival research and extensive *Drake-ing* in the west of England. I am deeply impressed by Susan's skilful transcription of *The Plymouth Black Book* and *The Widney Papers*. I had left the "easier" England chapters towards the end of the project, so I was delighted to follow her lead.

Documenting Drake in England lacks the adventures synonymous with those of the developing countries. However, the rich detail supplied by Susan, provided an exciting writing experience. The topographically intense text, almost makes me feel, as though Drake is still living amongst us.

John Thrower is a retired government scientist who also contacted me through the media. John's scientific approach enriched my sleuthing, when he joined me on three expeditions to Panamá. John has conducted an unprecedented scientific study on Drake's robbery of the Spanish mule train by publishing a book on the robbery site and the value of the treasure. John has enjoyed the honour of delivering an illustrated lecture to the prestigious Hakluyt Society, that has published much of the Drake primary sources. His original approach to Drakeology, included being photographed drinking Plymouth beer at Drake's anchorage in Costa Rica. This illustrated article appeared in the West of England regional press and in the Yorkshire Post. John frequently visits the lesser known Drake sites in England. John has drawn all the maps for this book and provides photographs for the cover for which I am deeply grateful.

I am indebted to now retired teacher of English, *Freda Mawson* who, during fifteen years of writing, corrected and coached my use of the written word.

I can modestly state that I am extremely proud of this book, because my amateurism has been moulded into professionalism by the aforementioned people. Collectively we have made this Drake book superlatively accurate, detailed and special.

left to right: Michael Turner, Susan Jackson, Raymond Aker, John Thrower

Chronology

1540	Drake born at Crowndale, Tavistock, Devon.
1566-7	sails in Captain Lovell's slave trading expedition.
1567-8	serves under John Hawkins in his 3rd slaving voyage.
1569	marries Mary Newman a seaman's daughter.
1570	reconnaissance voyage to Panamá.
1571	reconnaissance voyage to Panamá
1572-3	raids on Panamá and Colombia.
1575	serves under Earl of Essex in Ireland.
1577-80	Drake's great voyage of circumnavigation.
1581	knighted, mayor of Plymouth and purchased Buckland Abbey.
1583	Mary Newman dies.
1584	MP for Bossiney in north Cornwall.
1585	marries the wealthy Elizabeth Sydenham.
1585-6	plunders Cape Verde Islands, West Indies and Florida.
1587	attacks Cádiz and other Iberian towns.
1588	Vice Admiral of the Navy during the Spanish Armada.
1589	Lisbon expedition.
1590	fortifies Plymouth and St Nicholas Island
1591	Drake's leat conveys fresh water to Plymouth.
1593	MP for Plymouth.
1595-6	sails to the Canaries and the West Indies, laid to rest on 29 January.

Chapter One

Drake In England:
Birth to Adulthood

The Sources

Many of Drake's movements in England have been taken from
the standard biographies. Dr John Sugden has been the first
author to document thoroughly Drake's whereabouts. He has
uncovered new information concerning Drake's later life as a
civic leader and of his financial contributions towards public
works in Plymouth.

The passages in old English spelling have been kindly
transcribed by Susan Jackson as a result of her studying, *The
Plymouth Black Book, The Widney Papers and The Plymouth
Municipal Records - Collected Papers.* Susan explains,

"The miscellaneous collection of documents, gathered and
bound in a wooden cover overlaid with black leather, is aptly
known as *The Plymouth Black Book.* Principally, it contains
entries made by the mayors of Plymouth concerning the
important events of their respective annual sessions of duty.
However, the book is not complete. It also contains details of
property transactions in which the corporation were either
directly concerned or, acted as mediators in lawsuits.

The Widney Papers were found at Widney Court that once
stood in Plymouth. They are a record of the financial
transactions of the Plymouth Corporation during the 16th and
17th centuries. Unfortunately they are not complete in any one
year. Rather, they are random jottings - perhaps by the Council

Receiver for that year. Again, only the entries that directly or indirectly refer to Drake are cited. These include: formal entertaining by the corporation; errands; hire of transport; food and victual supplies; property transactions; building projects, because of Drake's later financial contributions; references to the leat, because of Drake's high profile involvement; defence projects; investment in Drake's voyages and supply of arms; the corporation's dealings with the Magistrates and Justices, because Drake was the Senior Magistrate and Justice, otherwise known as the Deputy Lord Lieutenant for the County of Devon."

"The Plymouth Municipal Records - Collected Papers is a miscellaneous collection of letters, leases, bills and other corporation records. They contain some material relating to Sir Francis Drake.

These corporation documents presented in rich and minuscule detail, begin to give us a fascinating insight into Drake's life as a member of Plymouth's civic and maritime community. This is the side of Drake that many biographies tend to under represent, as they understandably focus on Drake's maritime exploits.

The reader should note that, these documents date their years from Lady Day in April, rather than from 1 January. The retention of Elizabethan spelling and the Devonian variations, attest to the fact that, Sir Francis and his fellow mayors spoke with a rich West Country drawl. If you read these words aloud, the words are easy to comprehend!

These collections are housed at the West Devon Record Office at Coxside, Plymouth and can be viewed by prior appointment, or at their discretion on production of a small fee. They are some of the most fascinating documents that a historian can read."

The absence of full stops is not a modern omission. The explanations have been kindly supplied by Susan Jackson. Susan has ensured that, this is the first time that all the Plymouth Corporation Drake-related entries have been published in their entirety.

Tavistock, Devon

Francis, was the eldest of twelve sons fathered by Edmund Drake, a shearman. Author Harry Kelsey explains that this was a specialised job that required teasing the nap of the cloth and then trimming the nap with fine shears to make the surface as smooth as possible. This was performed at a fulling mill. Such

a mill stood a quarter of a mile down-river from Crowndale farm. Alternatively, Edmund probably performed the more common and less specialised job, that of shearing the sheep on his farm.

Francis was born in the parish of **Crowndale** a mile south of Tavistock. Kelsey extrapolates that Drake was most likely born in February or March 1540. The year was substantiated by: his cousin John, when he was interrogated by the Inquisition some forty years later; Drake's portrait on the Nicola van Sype World Map and by a Spanish judge in Cartagena.

The ancient market town of Tavistock lies on the western edge of the granite uplands of Dartmoor, on the banks of the River Tavy, from which the town derives its name. In 974 King Edgar chose Tavistock at which to build a Benedictine monastery. The abbey was rebuilt in stone. This stimulated the settlement of craftsmen and resultant commercial activity. Consequently, Henry I granted the town a weekly market and this isolated community became one of Devon's wealthiest and important towns. As a result of Henry VIII dissolving the monasteries, Tavistock Abbey surrendered its status on 3 March 1539. The buildings were stripped of all valuable commodities. In 1541 Buckland Abbey and its estate, four miles to the south, was sold to the Grenville family. However, Tavistock Abbey was not sold but granted to Lord John Russell, the President of the recently formed Council of the West. These councils administered the king's law in the remote regions of England. The Drake farm had been leased from the Abbey since 1441 by Francis's great great grandfather Henry, then to his son Simon in 1481 and to his son John 1520. This meant that Lord Russell became Edmund's father's landlord.

There were numerous Drakes living in Tavistock and
Whitchurch: many of whom were related. We know virtually
nothing about Drake's mother whose surname was Milwaye.
She had a brother called Richard. Drake's grandmother Margery
was a Hawkins. Her brother was Old William Hawkins, whose
sons were William and John. Hence, Edmund was their cousin.
Consequently, William and John were Francis's second
cousins. It was John Hawkins who was to be instrumental in
shaping Francis's career. There was a Drake family living on
both sides of the Tavy at Crowndale. East Crowndale fell
within the parish of Whitchurch. The Drakes of yeoman stock,
commanded an above average income and for generations,
probably lived in the same stone farmhouse. Remains of stone
foundations still exist on both sides of the Tavy. The two farms
were connected by a stone footpath which forded the river,
which is one of the fastest flowing in the country. Tradition
states that, Francis was born on the larger holding which was
on the west side, whilst Whitchurch folklore states otherwise.

However, since 1926 on the present Crowndale farmhouse wall there has been a plate claiming this to be near the site of Francis Drake's birthplace.

From Rixhill, there is a magnificent panoramic view of Crowndale Farm as one looks NW across the Tavy valley. With a wide angle lens, a picture can be composed to show the farmhouse in relation to Tavistock and the parish church.

Tradition claims that Francis Russell, who later became the Duke of Bedford and was the son and heir to Lord John Russell was Drake's godfather. Young Francis was named after him. This is substantiated by the fact that Francis was not a traditional Drake name. Since baptism records were not kept in Drake's time, we can only suppose that Francis was christened in the early 13th century St Eustachius Church.

In an attempt to document the christening, I also photographed the font in St Andrew's Church of Whitchurch.

Francis must have spent his first years being useful on his grandparent's farm, visiting the Friday market and numerous friends and relatives. Francis would have frequented **Whitchurch** and its church where his great uncle William Drake was vicar from 1524 to 1547. The church's history booklet documents William's period of service and states that he was buried inside the church. Perhaps young Francis attended the funeral. Another of his uncles was a school master in Whitchurch. In Tavistock, Drake would have witnessed the deterioration of the abbey. Even more of the abbey was destroyed when the Duke of Bedford ordered the centre of Tavistock to be remodelled in the 19th century. However, some of the abbey remains!

The abbey stood between the church and the river and ran parallel to both. In front of St Eustachius Church and within its grounds are the meagre remains of the cloisters. Across the road at the entrance to a hotel car park is the Abbot's Lodging, which is also known as Grimbal's Tower. The original entrance is on the south side of the wall. At the far end of the car park, down towards the river, is a well preserved tower. This is set within the same wall and is called the Still House. On the riverside of this wall is a long and beautiful walk as one passes between the river and the abbey wall. The scene is embellished by walking up-river when the Abbey Bridge comes into view. From this bridge, one obtains a timeless view of the Tavy and the abbey. A minute's walk to the north is the archway of Court Gate: the abbey's main entrance.

On 25 April 1548 Edmund with an accomplice, was indicted for assaulting and robbing a man of his purse in le Crose Lane at <u>Peter Tavy</u> and then stole a horse on which to escape. Edmund was fined. This must have undermined the family's standing in the tight-knit community. However, he was pardoned on the following 21 December.

Peter Tavy is situated four miles NE of Crowndale farm. The village still retains its church and a charming 12th century pub. To encapsulate the incident, I took a panoramic view looking NW towards these buildings, set in the typical beautiful, rolling, green hills of Devon.

Edward VI was now king and head of the Protestant Church of England. On Whitsunday in 1549 the use of a new prayer book was made compulsory in every church. The West Country Catholics rebelled violently. Edmund Drake stated that he wished to escape persecution and left Tavistock to begin a new life. This is the story which he told his sons. Later in life, Sir Francis relayed this account to contemporary historians, such as William Camden and John Stowe. However, according to Susan Jackson's study of the Lay Subsidiary Rolls for Tavistock, Edmund Drake left Tavistock in 1548. This suggests that Edmund urgently sought a fresh start before the rebellion.

Plymouth

The family took refuge in the Plymouth Castle Quadrate which overlooks the entrance to Sutton Pool harbour and on St Nicholas Island. This island is now called Drake's Island. A map drawn some forty years later, shows that St Michael's Church was the only substantial building on the island. Eventually Francis Drake's uncle Captain Richard Drake of Whitchurch shipped the family to the River Medway in Kent.

The Drakes probably chose Kent because here, Edmund and his wife had friends and relatives respectively. Friends included landowner John Fitz. His Fitzford estate bordered Crowndale and he also owned a mansion near Lewisham. The Fitz family was related to the Tremaynes of Tremeton Castle in Saltash. Another West Country family was the Mountjoys, who also held property SE of London. Francis was to enjoy the legacy of such old and prestigious inter-family connections.

Gillingham Reach, Kent

The Drakes lived in a hulk on the River Medway near the royal dockyard at Chatham, which was founded in 1547. Edmund earned a living preaching to the fleet. He formally educated his sons and much of his teaching was from the Bible. The sickly boy King Edward VI died and his Catholic half sister Mary became queen. Mary was half Spanish and intended to marry King Philip of Spain in order to re-cement the Catholic doctrine into the nation.

Rochester

In 1554 the Drakes witnessed another religious rebellion. This time it was Protestant and led by Thomas Wyatt, who made his headquarters in Rochester Castle. It was at Rochester Bridge where Wyatt made a stand against the queen's troops, whom he drove back to London along the Roman road of Watling Street. Nonetheless, all the rebels were executed and the royal marriage took place.

Drake would recognise parts of the Roman city today. Some of its walls survive. The Bridge Chapel for the disappeared 14th century bridge still remains. The Mediaeval walls enclose 23½ acres of pre-Drake historic treasures. Some of these walls can still be seen in the High Street. Rochester Castle is a fine example of a Norman castle. It features a seventy feet square, 113 feet high keep, which is the tallest in the country. Its walls are eleven to thirteen feet thick. Rochester Cathedral was consecrated in AD 604 and is the second oldest cathedral in England. The surviving Norman cathedral dates from 1080 and includes 12th and 14th century additions. The oldest parts are Gundulph's Tower and the crypt. Historians consider the crypt to be the finest in England. The castle walls were built in 1087 and the keep in 1127. The rebuilt St Margaret's Church has retained its 15th century tower. Several 16th century houses remain such as: Eastgate House, Restoration House, Satis House and Old Hall. Priors Gate is the best preserved out of the three remaining 14th century monastic gates. Six Poor

Travellers' House was a Tudor charity house founded by
Elizabethan MP Richard Watts, to provide travellers with one
night's accommodation. It is open Tuesday - Saturday
afternoons between 1 March and 31 October.

On the north bank of the Medway opposite Rochester, is the
ancient town of **Strood**. The pre-Drake buildings which Francis
could have seen include, the All Saints Church, which is over
900 years old with its fine Mediaeval wall paintings and St
Nicholas Church in Strood High Street. The nave was rebuilt
between 1812-14 but the original Mediaeval tower remains. On
Knight Road is the 13th century Hall House of Temple Manor,
built by the Knight Templars to provide lodgings for the
crusading knights.

Drake was witness to one of the most violent religious
upheavals this country has ever known. Under Queen Mary,
Edmund would have lost his job and would be desperate for his
sons to supplement the family income. The move from a farm
house to a hulk, was instrumental in Francis, John, Joseph and
Thomas becoming sailors instead of farmers. From the age of
ten or twelve, Francis was apprenticed to the owner of a small
coastal bark. Young Francis was being schooled in seamanship
as the vessel frequented the east coast ports. Drake later told
Camden that he, *"sometimes transported Merchandise into
France and Zeland."* [Wagner, 317] Any merchant vessel
sailing from the Medway would have traded with: **La
Rochelle, Le Harve, Calais, Antwerp, Flushing** and **Brill**. In
SE England young Francis would have docked at the seven
Cinque Ports of: **Hastings, Winchelsea, Hythe, Romney,
Sandwich, Dover** and **Rye**. These ports were strategically
placed to defend the realm against periodic attacks from the
French. Consequently, Edward I awarded these towns a charter.

They were exempted from tax and were granted autonomy, in exchange for ships and seamen when naval defence required. By the 14th century, Rye was a full Head Port.

Rye, East Sussex

Thirteenth century storms changed the configuration of the coastline, to form a large and safe harbour in front of the medieval town, that stood on top of a sandstone hill. Henry VIII protected the harbour by building Camber Castle on its west shore. Ships could anchor right under the town. Consequently, with the increased shipping the port became extremely prosperous. In Tudor times, Rye became one of England's most important ports. Elizabeth's visit testified to its status.

Due to the town's unusual hilltop setting, the town is very popular with the thinking traveller who appreciates the intense cluster of buildings that date from the 14th century. Drake's world is very much in evidence. Rye Castle overlooks the former harbour. Its garden still contains a seaward trained cannon. By walking a hundred metres along a typical cobbled street, one reaches the 12th century church of St Mary that was rebuilt between 1500 and 1600. Both edifices offer magnificent roof top views of the town and countryside. On the NE side of the town is the Landgate that was built in 1329. It is the only remaining of the four gates along the town's walls.

An encompassing view of the town from the SE can be secured from the south bank of the River Rother, that nowadays, flows in front of the town. Due to three centuries of silting, the sea is two miles away. Therefore one has to walk a mile across fields to reach Camber Castle. These distances give a clear impression of the harbour's original size.

Winchelsea

As with Rye, storms struck the town in the 13th century. However, its destruction caused it to be moved and reconstructed on the present-day steep-sided hill. The rebuild with its 720 households was completed in 1292. The new town supported two shipwrights, several ships' caulkers and fishermen. By 1600 the sea had receded causing the narrowing and silting up of the river channel. Like Rye, the town stands a few miles inland. Drake could have seen the 13th century Strand Gate and St Thomas's Church.

Hoo & Upnor, Kent

When aboard the bark in the Medway, Francis would have seen a church and fort which still defy the passage of time. At Hoo on the north shore of Gillingham reach is the 13th century St Werburgh Church with its imposing, yet elegant shingled spire.

Chatham dockyard began its life in 1547 and under Elizabeth was assuming greater importance. Consequently, in 1559 a turreted gun fort was built at Upnor on the north bank of the Medway to protect the shipping from attack. Drake would have witnessed its construction. Little did he realise, that he was to build five forts on smaller lines around the world and design and oversee the construction of Plymouth's star-shaped fort.

Upchurch

Elizabeth ascended the throne in 1558 and was a Protestant from political expediency. By personal inclination she was High Anglican. She disapproved of Protestantism as she did of Catholicism. On 25 January 1561, Edmund Drake became vicar of nearby Upchurch until his death in 1567. After a hard life at sea, young Francis would have no doubt enjoyed the comforts of the new family home at Upchurch Vicarage.

Francis must have impressed his bachelor captain, because when he died, he bequeathed Francis the bark. For a few more years, young Drake continued plying his trade. Queen Elizabeth's long and glorious reign was to be synonymous with maritime expansion. Drake would have heard about the West Country ports being in the vanguard of this exciting development. The ambitious young Francis saw this as his chance to gain ocean-going sailing experience and to share in the acquisition of the fabulous riches from the transatlantic trade with the New World.

Plymouth

Probably in 1564, Drake sold his bark and returned to Plymouth to join John Hawkins whose family had long been at the forefront in fitting out armed merchant ships. Contrary to Howes and secondary writer Kelsey, Drake was not raised by the Hawkins family but entered their employ as a young adult.

North East Spain

According to contemporary chronicler Edmund Howes, [Wagner, 305] who was writing from hearsay, master merchant mariner Drake, was made purser, hence, a junior officer on a Hawkins sponsored voyage to Biscay in 1558. No details of this short voyage have emerged, except that Drake converted a Welsh Catholic named, Michael Morgan or Morgan Gilbert to the Protestant faith. Howes states that when Drake was two years older, he sailed to Guinea and two years later was commanding the *Judith*. However Drake commanded the *Judith* in 1567-8. Therefore Drake may have gained transatlantic experience at a younger age than is commonly thought. Hence, the Biscay date could be wrong. We do not know what year Drake sold his bark and sought his fortune with the Hawkins family in Plymouth. Sugden suggests 1564 because it closely precedes the departure of the 1566 Hawkins sponsored Lovell voyage, when Drake's movements become definite.

Chapter Two

The Slaving Voyage of 1567-8

with reference to the 1566-7 Lovell slaving voyage

The Sources

The English narratives are by John Hawkins, Miles Philips - Hawkins's 13 year old page boy, Job Hortop a Lincolnshire-bred gunner and the anonymous author of *The Cotton Narrative*. They are in general agreement and the first three have been re-printed by Hakluyt. Richard Hakluyt was a famous Elizabethan travel writer who published the accounts of many contemporary and earlier voyages. He gleaned further information through personal contact with the likes of Drake and Hawkins.

True Declaration of the troublesome Voyage of Mr John Hawkins to the Parts of Guinea and the West Indies in the years of our Lord 1567 and 1568. This is the official report and was published in 1569. It is only 1,300 words in length. Hawkins has omitted many events and much detail.

A discourse written by one Miles Philips. This narrative is also of 1,300 words and suffers from being written in retrospect. The voyage facts are accurate but brief. It was composed after 1583 when Philips arrived in England escaping from Spanish custody. Philips, Hortop and others, had volunteered to be left behind in México after the disaster at San Juan de Ulua, when there was not enough food and water for the homeward voyage.

The travailes of Job Hortop were first published in 1591, a year after his return to England. Being of 2,500 words, it is the most detailed of the three published by Hakluyt. Hortop is guilty of chronological and geographical inaccuracies. Besides writing from memory, his recall was clouded due to the repetitive experiences in Guinea-Bissau. Here the larger ships kept clear of the shore, whilst Hortop and company scoured the rivers for slaves. All the mangrove-lined rivers looked identical and some of the rivers have been named in the wrong order. For example, Hortop wrote that after leaving Sierra Leone, they went to the River Grande, where he described an event which occurred at the San Domingos river two months earlier! Hortop was more disposed to recording vivid details of the strange animals and plants.

The longest, detailed and systematic account of this voyage, is the 22,000 word Cotton MSS., Otho E viii, ff. 17-41b in the British Museum. Due to a fire at the Cotton Library in 1731, the top outer words have been destroyed. According to Hawkins's main biographer, J. A. Williamson, it's author was most probably Valentine Green because when he was taken prisoner he used similar phrases in his deposition. This is the official narrative of the voyage. It also contains transcriptions of Hawkins's letters to the Spanish officials when desiring a trading licence. This suggests that it was written in Hawkins's cabin and has been published by Williamson.

The Portuguese accounts which deal with the raid on Cacheu, Guinea-Bissau are lodged at the Public Records Office in London. Irene Wright published, *Spanish Documents Concerning English Voyages to The Caribbean*. She collected a host of Spanish dispatches, written by colonial officials, that report upon the Caribbean leg of this, and the Lovell voyage. Her other cited Spanish narratives are compiled from the English captives in México, for example, Robert Barrett's deposition, but add little to the record. These are housed in the Mexico City archives. All have been cited by secondary author Rayner Unwin, who has written the first book that deals exclusively and in great detail with this voyage.

The evidence of the West African leg is thus often retrospective, repetitive, chronologically dislocated and geographically tenuous. This was the foundation upon which my expeditions tried to illuminate pictorially, the fragments of Drake's, short and peripheral involvement in the slave trade.

Introduction: The New World

In 1566 Drake was an officer under Captain John Lovell. This Hawkins sponsored voyage sailed from Plymouth on 9 November 1566 and would introduce Drake to the slave trade. Hawkins's first two slaving voyages of 1562 and 1564 had produced enormous profits that had been gained amidst difficulty. Therefore an outline of the geographical and political context is required.

When Colombus discovered the New World in 1492, Rome predicted that disputes of territorial claims would arise between the principal European maritime powers of Spain and Portugal. In 1493 Pope Alexander VI divided the New World between Spain and Portugal by drawing a north to south line 370 leagues west of the Cape Verde Islands; half-way between the Azores and West Indies. Colombus thought he had discovered Asia, hence it was an arbitrary line as nobody knew which sector of the world would become the richer. All territories west of the line would belong to Spain. This would be the mineral rich lands of Central and South America, where the world would become Spanish speaking. Seven years later east of the line, Brazil was discovered, and became a massive area of South America to be ruled by the Portuguese tongue. The two imperialist powers peacefully met in the Far East. By sailing west, Spain had reached the Philippines and the Portuguese, via the Cape of Good Hope, had colonised the Spice Islands in modern-day Indonesia.

Spain's interests in its new found colonies were: religious, political and economic. King Philip had banned ships from Protestant nations from entering his ports and ordered the colonists not to trade with these heretic interlopers. The English and French merchants resented being excluded from such a rich and enormous area of God's Earth. They opposed the Pope's right to divide the world into such a trading duopoly, that eventually would widen the balance of power between the Catholic and Protestant nations to the detriment of the latter. England needed to grow economically from this trade and thus eliminate, or reduce Spain's subsequent military threat. In reality, the struggling and isolated colonial settlements needed Hawkins's slaves because Spain's supply ships could not keep pace with the colonists' requirements. The settlers reported, that for every one supply ship, there were four interlopers. Therefore trade occurred unofficially or Hawkins encouraged the officials to report that he had forced them to trade with his superior military power.

On Hawkins's third slaving voyage, he was accompanied by the young Francis Drake. The latter had returned within a month from the Lovell voyage. This had been Drake's first voyage beyond European waters. Few details of the venture were

18

recorded. One noteworthy fact, is that a Michael Morgan sailed on both voyages. Morgan was tortured in 1574. He confessed that on the Lovell voyage, he was converted to Protestantism by Francis Drake. For the sake of convenience, the existing fragments of the Lovell expedition, will be juxtaposed to the Hawkins voyage. Essentially, all of the Hawkins voyages frequented the same ports. Provisions and water were collected in the Canaries. Slaves were captured on the West African coast and sold to the Spanish colonists in the Caribbean, where their innate strength was required in the silver mines, and to work on the plantations in the oppressive, humid heat, accentuated by the blazing sun.

The expedition was financed on a joint-stock basis. The queen provided two ships. The Hawkins family supplied the remaining vessels. Contributions were received from merchant investors.

Cattewater, Plymouth, England

To prepare for the voyage, Hawkins's fleet was anchored in the Cattewater. During late August, seven Spanish ships sailed right into this inner deep water haven without dipping their flags and furling their top sails. To compound this mark of nautical disrespect, they intended to arrogantly "rub noses" with the English ships by anchoring alongside. Consequently, Hawkins's cannons raked the hulls of the leading vessels. The audacious visitors went about, effected a belated salute and anchored in the lee of St. Nicholas Island. A formal complaint was lodged. Hawkins received a letter from the queen, forbidding him to take such high-handed action in her name. During these early September days of diplomatic ramifications, Drake joined the fleet. According to the deposition of Morgan

Jillert, a Welshman, to be captured in México, Drake was aboard the *Jesus*. After a service in St Andrew's Church attended by the 400 crew and officers, the fleet spread its canvas on 2 October.

I wanted a view of Plymouth from the Cattewater. I went to Turnchapel and was pleased to see a marina, which really facilitated picture taking. Along a network of pontoons, I was able to reach the outermost position, that was nearly in mid-channel. I gained much appreciated elevation by boarding a brigantine. The resultant picture simulated Drake's unhindered view of Plymouth where the fleet was anchored and as it made sail.

Cape Finisterre, Spain

Three days out, Hawkins instructed his captains to rendezvous at Santa Cruz in Tenerife if they should be divided by adverse weather. On the fourth day, *"...an extreeme storme then tooke us neere unto Cape Finister..,* [Philips, Hakluyt, Vol. VI. 297] the ships were put asunder by a storm lasting for four days.

In 1991, I had reached a point one mile to the SW of the cape in a hired boat from the harbour of Finisterre and had managed to reduce the initial asking price from 5,000 to 2,000 pesetas. The green and rocky tip of the cape was devoid of trees. The view was restricted by low cloud that enveloped its higher levels. My disappointment was eased by the thought that on this voyage, Drake must have also seen a partially obscured cape. However, on later voyages, he must have enjoyed clear views. This meant that I had to make a return visit.

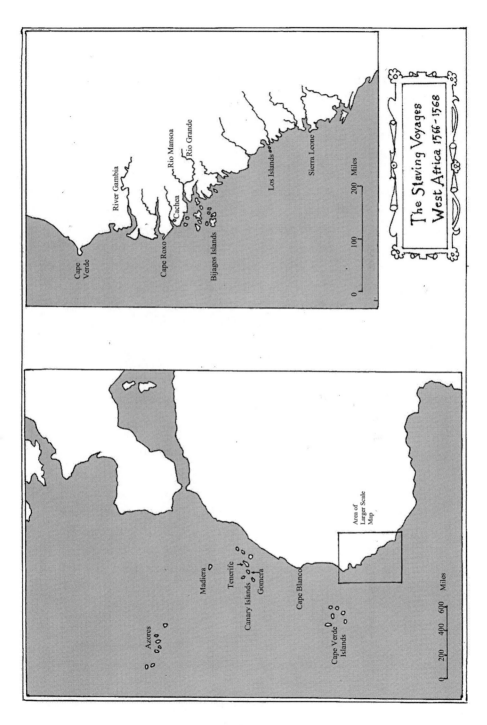

The Slaving Voyages
West Africa 1566 - 1568

River Gambia

Cape Verde

Cape Roxo

Cachea

Rio Mansoa

Rio Grande

Bijagos Islands

Los Islands

Sierra Leone

0   100   200   Miles

Azores

Madiera

Tenerife

Canary Islands

Gomera

Cape Blanco

Cape Verde Islands

Area of Larger Scale Map

0   200   400   600   Miles

Santa Cruz and Bufadero, Tenerife, Canary Islands

Hawkins dispatched a messenger to the governor explaining that he wished to gather his fleet, purchase provisions and to water. Amid the diplomatic courtesies, Hawkins sent presents ashore and banqueted the officials. Despite the harmonious overtones, the shrewd Hawkins declined an invitation to go ashore. The Spanish sources confirm that the hosts considered Hawkins as a common pirate. What follows from *The Cotton Narrative* gives credence to his intuition.

During the night on the fourth day, the Spaniards moved all their shipping that was anchored between the fort's guns and the English fleet. Hawkins knew that his fleet lay at the mercy of the Spanish artillery and suspected their motives. At midnight, Hawkins relocated his ships, *"...ij leagues from the towne, and neverthelesse all this ankered there, sent his boat ashore to another place, and drave of the tyme filling water."* [Williamson, 501]

During the watering, Spanish officials boarded the flagship, enquiring why Hawkins had suddenly dispensed with their hospitality. Simultaneously, the watering party were summoned aboard. *"...oure generall comaunded to waye, and thus as we passed by the town... and departed towardes Adessia, another place in the ilond, where after we had ridden one day..."* the *Judith* which had been sent to Gomera, brought news that the *Minion*, the *William and John* and the *Swallow* were waiting. [ibid]

From my 1986 visit, I had deduced that the fort was the one that stands at the water's edge, south of the city centre, and that the watering occurred at Tabaiba Cove. The latter is en route: five miles to the south and corresponds with the stated distance.

However, I procured *The Cotton Narrative* three years after my visit. The above quotation suggests that water was taken to the north of the town. Furthermore, I had learnt of the Adessia anchoring. To locate the former would require examination of the Spanish sources. To find the bay meant consulting ancient maps, as the bay's name no longer exists. Furthermore, it may have been mistranslated from the Spanish sounding of the name, just like Hawkins and Drake were sometimes written as Acles and Draque.

I met with the librarian, Sr. Juan Gómez Pamo in the Canary Museum, Las Palmas. In a book that dealt with pirates who frequented the Canaries, Hawkins was given great prominence. There was a photograph, that was taken during the early part of this century of the San Cristóbal fort, that had threatened Hawkins's ships. Water lapped against its walls. I was informed that it no longer stands and that its site is now occupied by the monument to those who fell during the Spanish Civil War.

My diplomatic letter was crucial for obtaining the post office roof top view across the monument, looking towards Hawkins's second anchorage. I had carefully combed through the Spanish text of this intellectual book and made this second personal discovery to add to the English history books.

"John Hawkins cuyo recelo había ido creciendo día a día dispuso entonces que los navios se distanciasen algo más, situándose frente a la montaña del Bufadero para estar abrigo de todo riesgo."

[*Piraterias y Ataques Navales Contra Las Islas Canarias*, Tomo 1[Vol. 1] Antonio Rumeu, El Consejo Superior de Investigaciones Cientificas, Instituto Jeronimo Zurita, Madrid, 1946, 435]

Translated it reads that, Hawkins became more wary by the day and moved his ships adjacent to Mount Bufadero. This was truly revelational information. The mountain is barely at half the stated distance and is indeed, northwards of the city. The Bufadero river valley runs up into the mountain. Residents of Bufadero hamlet stated that water flows during January and February. Hawkins however, could have taken water from the wells, that are the island's source of water. A harbour breakwater runs along where Hawkins would have anchored. My diplomatic reference was used as the last means of persuasion, in securing an elevated view of the coastline from an oil tanker. Dock installations now cover the original landing site. The imposing mountainous valley sides, still render a view that Hawkins and Drake would recognise. Despite the overwhelming presence of 20th century structures, I felt compensated by the uncovering of this topographical information and on this occasion, left Santa Cruz with all the answers.

"Adessia Bay," Tenerife

I was impressed by the librarian's ease in providing detailed and positive answers to my questions. The old Spanish spelling was *Adexe* and is now **Adeje**. It takes its name from the town on the island's west coast, two miles inland, eight miles N of its most SW point. The anchorage is forty-five miles SW of Santa Cruz. From a hired boat, I could see the landing beach at Adeje cove and the town on the lower slopes under the towering peak of Teide volcano.

Despite the official line, there were some Spanish merchants who benefited from Hawkins's visits. It is well documented in Spanish history books, that Hawkins enjoyed commercial relations with Pedro de Ponte who lived in Adeje. The two might have met whilst Hawkins waited for news that his missing ships were at Gomera.

San Sebastián, Gomera

One can easily follow Drake's wake by taking the *Ferry Gomera* from nearby Los Cristianos to San Sebastián. The 21 mile crossing takes 1½ hours. I presented my credentials to the *Ferry Gomera* harbour office. After telephoning the head office, I was issued with a free return ticket. On board, I was permitted to take pictures from the bridge.

The English accounts do not name the town but since Hawkins was greeted by the governor, who willingly furnished supplies, this suggests that this was at the island's capital town of San Sebastián.

From the *Leicester Journal*, [131] compiled on Drake's 1585 voyage, we learn more about the island.

"...they say there is but one towne in all the Illand, and in that one castell but indifferently fortefyed, the which we could not see. neyther can it be verye rich because it is sclenderly inhabited."

25

Finally, illustrations in Spanish books show that Hawkins frequented San Sebastián because the governor had more autonomy.

The town lies at the mouth of a steep valley, which has dictated the limits of its growth. It is protected from the NE Trades by two high, brown, barren, volcanic, rocky headlands, that plunge vertically into the deep blue sea. Drake would have stepped on to the black sandy beach, that turns into gravel and pebbles. San Sebastián is a modern port-town. The only remaining relic from the 16th century, that Drake could have seen, is the fortified tower called Torre del Conde, to which the *Leicester Journal* may have referred.

After two days, on 4 November, *"Oure generall gave him thankes, and after he had fullie watred here..."* the sails were hoisted for Cape Blanc. [The Cotton Narrative, 502] The reunited fleet was carried by a wind-whipped seething blue sea, speckled with white crests, that plumed beneath an empty blue sky.

Cape Blanc, Mauritania

Upon arrival, three Portuguese ships were found abandoned because nearly three weeks earlier a French fleet had raided this fishing outpost, causing the Portuguese to flee to an inland castle. Hawkins exercised his legal right and claimed the ships. Hawkins summoned their owners, informing them that he was to keep only one. Fifteen days were spent careening, enjoying the world's richest fishing and preparing the Portuguese caravel.

Cape Verde, Senegal

This name also applies to the nine mile seaward end of the Cape Verde peninsula between Point des Almadies and Cap Manuel to the south. Almadies is Africa's most westerly point. Approaching from the north, the sailor sees flat land but three miles southward, the two knolls of Les Mamelles form a striking contrast. These peaks are 74 and 105 metres high. Their French name aptly applies to a woman's chest. During the rainy season, the knolls are decorated with stunted bushes and trees. For the early European sailors who had rolled back the unknown frontiers by skirting the Sahara coast, this part of the peninsula soon earned the name "Green Cape". The knolls were detailed and made available for other English sailors in 1566 by George Fenner during his voyage to Guinea.

"...two small round hils, seeming to us about a league one from the other, which is the Cape, and betweene them are a great store of trees, and in all our dayes sailing we saw no land so high..." [Hakluyt, Vol. IV. 143]

Cape Verde became a notable landmark. This refreshing semi - "green" cape at the southern edge of the barren Sahel, enabled seamen to re-establish their position. The pioneering seamen knew that the cape was a nautical sign post, that pointed due west for the Cape Verde Islands and the Caribbean. Arbitrarily and conveniently, it divided the Arab Barbary coast from the Guinea coast of Black Africa to the south. Here Hawkins commenced searching for slaves.

"...we came to anker harde by the Cape..." [Cotton Narrative, 503] *"...in twelve fadome water;"* [Philips, op. cit. 297] This does not necessarily mean adjacent to the present-day

Mamelles hill lighthouse. Mysteriously, the cape's point is three miles NW of this landmark called Cape Verde by Fenner and as shown on modern charts being on the peninsula of Cape Verde. Unwin, [76 & 79] surmises that, Hawkins landed in the lee of a small island before rounding the cape. This would be at N'gor Island which protects a small basin. Due to reefs, the fleet would have anchored at its entrance in the still, seaward waters of the island, which is in the lee of the NE Trades. Here four cables NW of the W end of the island, adjacent to the basin's entrance, The *Africa Pilot Vol. 1* notes a good anchorage. Its depth of 22 metres corresponds with Philips's twelve fathoms. To anchor any further south, ships need to stand further out to sea to avoid the heavy west swell, that rolls into the bays to the south of Les Mamelles. On this visit, I hired a boat and pictured this anchorage from a seaward approach with views of the knoll of Mamelles. By land, I surveyed the coast as far south as Magdeleine Island, where the beaches are fewer and less protected. Due to a lack of contemporary geographical detail, we have to rely upon the comprehensive descriptions from the sailing directions. They state that the best landing beach on the peninsula is at N'gor village. This sandy beach is on the basin's south side, facing N'gor Island. Its 15 metre elevation could have been used to conceal Hawkins's ships to the seaward of the island, since he intended to surprise a Negro village early next morning.

According to Philips, the village lay six miles up country. As the inhabitants fled, the 200 English were repelled with toy-like bows and arrows, the size of which amused the interlopers as they plucked the pin-like arrow heads from their skin.

Ironically, the tips had been dipped in poison and two days later, over twenty men were bearing the symptoms of what we now know as lockjaw. Sticks were used to keep mouths open. Hawkins who was hit in the left arm, saved himself. He used a clove of garlic to extract the poison from the wound - a lesson that he had learnt from a Negro. Nine days later, eight of the injured died: a high price for only nine captives.

In the Senegambia Museum, Banjul, Gambia, I photographed bows and arrows ranging from long bows to diminutive versions, that were no larger than a coat hanger! To add spice to the African flavour, I included drums, that the English would have seen in various villages. It is impossible to reconstruct Hawkins's encounter because there are no longer bush-mud huts this far north, since the Sahel has encroached southwards and the once rustic setting has been diluted by commercial tourism and the nearness of Dakar. To outline the raid, I climbed the knoll at Cape Verde to view the entire cape peninsula, with its off-shore islands and the surrounding flat, now semi -"verde" landscape. Prior to purchasing and reading the sailing directions in 1991, I had been to the cape twice. This subsequent study, had reassuringly confirmed my earlier observations, that could now be expressed in more positive wording, such as that N'gor beach was more than likely where Hawkins had landed.

The fleet sailed south and another life was regrettably lost, when a man fell overboard.

The River Gambia

This is the first navigable river in Black West Africa. The four mile wide estuary, must have been quite a sight for the less travelled seamen. Its banks were lined with Negro villages. After the disaster at Cape Verde, Hawkins would have welcomed swift compensation. The river was not penetrated because the natives would have braced themselves due to the presence of six French ships anchored near the bar; two of which joined Hawkins for a share in the anticipated profits, increasing his sail to nine. Both fleets remained at anchor for a day to reorganise, during which time, young Drake was given his first command. According to Hortop, he became captain of a Portuguese bark, the *Grace of God* that the French had seized at Cape Blanc. Philips states that Drake was in command of a fifty ton bark, the *Judith*. Of the latter, we have no record until Drake was in the Caribbean.

The scene was captured by a wide angle lens from the deck of the Barra to Banjul ferry, which provided a near free and convenient platform. Due to the width of the estuary and its low banks, the view was bland.

"8 leagues to the northward of Cabo Roxo"

According to *The Cotton Narrative*, during light airs, a landing was made when Negroes were seen near the water's edge. The landing party tried to entice the natives with trinkets and asked to be shown water. However, they fled. Drake in his role of captain, probably did not go ashore to slave hunt.

Eight leagues equals twenty-four statute miles. Hence, the landing was on the beach in the Casamance region of Senegal. The proximity of the Casamance river, would have denoted habitation. The whole coastline from Casamance to Cape Roxo is low. It comprises many long yellow, sandy beaches, that are broken only by earth-rock headlands near Cap Skirring. Green fields with low trees form a repetitive backdrop. Since we are not given any geographical descriptions, the stated distance, with an error of say four miles, prevents an exact identification. Since the beach is virtually continuous, the pictures are at worst, almost identical to the original scene.

During my first visit, the photography had been based upon the secondary works of Unwin, who does not state the distance given in *The Cotton Narrative*. To represent the story, I chose the beach at Cap Skirring for its easy access. The late addition of *The Cotton Narrative* to my expanding Drake library had proved costly. Cap Skirring is only ten miles north of Cape Roxo. However, the typical scenic qualities of the beach were enhanced by clusters of wood-reed huts, situated where the beach and vegetation merge. Nonetheless, I needed to stand as close as possible to the landing site. Since I needed to return to West Africa, I forced myself to return to Ziguinchor, but this time by air at a cost of £100. To add gloom to this irksome, time consuming task, upon my arrival, it was pouring with rain.

On the plane, I met a French couple, whose packaged holiday included an hour's taxi ride to Cap Skirring. I managed to tag-along for free. The greedy taxi driver considered me as an extra source of revenue. The holiday village owner, M. Christian Jacquot explained that he had chartered the vehicle and the number of passengers was irrelevant. When the argument was won, I exploited this man's ability to help others. I displayed all my credentials.

M. Jacquot recognised my status as a shoestring researcher and that I had come all this way just for one picture! To my delight, I was given free accommodation in tropical rustic luxury. During the rain, time was as usual, spent studying and writing, whilst my host arranged boat hire for the following day, since he could negotiate a far cheaper price. It transpired that the fishermen worked for him and that all I had to pay for was the fuel. Admittedly, I arrived a few minutes late and the fishermen had already left. No other boats were available. Luckily, M. Jacquot supplied me with a driver and a four-wheeled jeep, after it had dawned upon me that we may be able to reach the landing place by the beach. We traversed the first ten kilometres along a mud trail to Diembéreng village. The next ten, were along the unbroken, yellow beach. All the way, I had prayed for no obstructions and bright light. When obstacles appeared in the form of trees, the <u>River Casamance</u> was in sight and the jeep's trip metre denoted that only a short walk was required to ensure that my footprints would cross those of whom had landed. The beach was inhabited by small, white crabs, which were somewhat camera shy. The shoreline was of low dunes, covered with an ivy-like vine and occasional trees. The scene was as featureless as their encounter but had to be included for the thoroughness of the Drake archive. A simulated landing shot was achieved by standing up to my neck in the stormy sea. I left Senegal, knowing that this third visit was the last.

Cape Roxo, Guinea-Bissau

Hawkins brushed past the Bay of Sucujaque. Its northern curving shore is protected by the sandy cape. The point is flat but the cape steadily rises northwards to around five metres of dunes, which are held firm by grass and bushes. The cape is still a well known landmark. It is where the north to south running coast swings south-east towards Liberia. For Hawkins, it was also the gateway to the most fertile slaving ground, where the coast largely consists of mangrove swamps pierced by estuaries up to seven miles wide. Henceforth, the deep draft vessels remained anchored off the estuaries, while the light draft boats repetitively searched the seemingly identical rivers.

Contrary to popular local opinion, I was able to reach the cape by walking several miles along a deserted beach. The southern end of the cape is in Guinea-Bissau. Boat hire for the ten mile excursion, was too costly. The fishermen wanted the "tourist" to make them "flush" overnight. They justified a charge of £50 because it would require crossing the border, which could be patrolled by curious soldiers. From a boat, the flat, boring and curving shore could not be photographically encapsulated. However, with the cape in the foreground, shots of the sweeping bay did provide a graphic view. It was easy to picture Hawkins's ships punctuating the vast seascape.

Cacheu

Near Cape Roxo, Hawkins had learnt from an intercepted Portuguese caravel, of a slaving station up the River San Domingos, fifteen miles southward. Hawkins anchored outside its bar. The caravel was forced to pilot the *Angel*, two pinnaces and a party of forty men, commanded by twenty-five year old Robert Barrett from Saltash, fifteen miles up the straight and one mile wide river to Cacheu. Six Portuguese ships emerged through the Harmattan haze. Barrett's request to trade was received with gunfire. He chose to attack rather than seek reinforcements. With effective fire power, he rapidly approached the caravels during their reloading phase. The defenders fled. To Barrett's disappointment, there were no slaves on board. Meanwhile, the fleet remained in the estuary.

"The next morning M. Francis Drake with his carvel, the Swallow, *and the* William and John *came into the river, with captaine Dudley and his souldiers, who landed being but a hundred soldiers,"* [Hortop, in Hakluyt, Vol. VI. 338] *The Cotton Narrative* states a total of 240 men who now marched *"...to spoyle a towne which was abowt a myle from the water side where oure shippes did lie to see if he cowde take any negros there".* [506] As the settlement was being fired - under Portuguese orders - a multitude of Negroes arose from the *"fieldes"*. The English retreated to the river, suffering only light casualties. An example of the Negro stoutness was recorded in *The Cotton Narrative*. A native pursued the fleeing

row boats. He seized an oar and, despite an arrow passing through him he swam ashore and carrying the oar, ran forty paces along the river bank to seaward before dropping dead.

Present-day Cacheu village is situated on the river bank, where stands a well preserved 15th century Portuguese fort. The accounts do not mention this. One hundred metres up-river, is the remains of a jetty. To avoid the soft mud at low water, it is likely that a wooden landing stage existed on or near this spot during the raid, to which the English made fast their skiffs on this tidal stretch of river.

Photographically, the wharf comprised the foreground, whilst views up-river, across the river and the river mouth formed the background. From a dugout canoe, all embracing approaching views were secured. I was prevented from taking a square-on view, of the village centre, off which, Drake might have anchored. The Police arrested me as I was about to be taken out in a canoe for the second phase. Since I had hidden the roll of film, I only surrendered the newly started roll. I had to be content with 80% of the possible angles. My timetable prevented a return visit, where I would once again face a ridiculous charge for a mile boat ride. This was because the few white visitors gladly pay £5 per night at the small hotel, which is the national wage for two weeks' work. This seemed to cause some resentment. A few days later, a high ranking official from the province, told the Honorary British consulate, that the arrest and confiscation of film was unnecessary. He stated that local attitudes had to change if tourism was to be promoted.

I was released after an hour but still had not studied the route of Barrett's attack on the village. Defiantly and hastily, from a mile inland, I pictured the lush fields looking along the road towards the river.

Seven years later, I returned to Cacheu to rectify the photographic deficiency. Attitudes had changed, partially due to Don Pepe. This Spaniard was building a fish factory: 150 metres west of the fort. Pepe had restored the former hotel and gave me food and accommodation. Upon seeing a homeward bound canoe, I scrambled through knee deep mud, where I cut my foot. I enthusiastically hired the service of these three boys. The westerly views were unfortunately backlit. However, I had attained all the seaborne angles for just $3.

My ultimate objective was to position myself in the estuary. That night, Pepe's French assistant, Dominique, enlisted the help of the fishing co-ordinator, who brought along the fisherman who resided next door. The excursion would cost $80. With the sun in the east, I now ideally completed the Cacheu views.

I had no chart but the national map showed that it was fifteen miles to the estuary. The canoe covered about ten miles an hour. Hence, we took under two hours to arrive. The north shore of the estuary was broken by two tributaries. The south shore projected more to seaward. The view up-river was as I had imagined. Pictures comprised a vast expanse of flat, grey sea, bordered in the hazy distance by two dark green, flat, tree and mangrove clad banks. Along with the east coast of the USA; this was Drake's least photogenic anchorage. However, sailing along this lonely river in Drake's wake was nonetheless, a gratifying experience.

River Mansoa

From a ferry, thirty-five miles further south-east, this river was recorded forty miles up stream, where it is nearly a mile wide! This was yet another river lined with mangrove swamps, along which I felt the Hawkins expedition had passed.

"Rio Grande"

Unravelling the confusing order of events in the *Hortop* and the *Cotton Narratives*, enables us to substantiate that here, Hawkins purchased a much needed bark for slave hunting. This grand river is now called the **Gêba**. Its seven mile wide estuary is the widest in West Africa.

"...we past the time upon the coast of Guinea, searching with all diligence the rivers from Rio Grande, unto Sierra Leona, till the twelfth of Januarie, in which time we had not gotten together a hundreth and fiftie Negros:"
[Hawkins, Hakluyt, Vol. VII. 54]

I could visualise the English easily capturing Negroes in their dugouts but I was unclear as to how they were captured ashore. Furthermore, I needed to record their largely unchanged way of life. For the equivalent of 23 pence, I caught the daily ferry from Bissau to Enxudé on the south bank. It was twelve miles up river and a rewarding experience. A typically rare landing bank interrupted the mangrove swamp. The inland was flat, open ground, well cultivated and dotted with huge trees, underneath the shade of which, were clusters of primitive huts. Fences linked the dwellings together, which I perceived were designed to keep livestock in and wild animals out. During darkness, it would have been easy to surround each cluster of huts. By their own design, the inhabitants would have been hemmed in as victims of their own success.

Exploring each cluster, was like meandering through a time capsule. Apart from the occasional tin or plastic bucket, there was no evidence of the twentieth century. The people slept on sacks stuffed hard with straw, inside their circular dingy huts of mud with reed roofs. Their self-sufficiency was evident. All the food was grown in the neighbouring fields, or in some cases, the spacious areas between a hut and the curved wicker fence. Some clusters of huts were purely for livestock. Agricultural and domestic work was aided by hand crafted wooden implements. During the day, the men worked the fields, whilst the bare breasted women tended to their babies and prepared food. A community spirit of sharing ensured survival. An Italian Padre told me that these people are pure and best left to practise their own religion.

Bijagos Islands

The estuaries now overlooked the offshore Bijagos archipelago. They consist of at least twenty flat, tree covered islands, surrounded by shifting sandbanks. Upon leaving the *River Grande*, Hawkins with his deep draft ships, gave these islands a wide berth to seaward. He may have sent some of the smaller craft to landward to search more rivers. Others could have passed between the islands seizing the few Negroes who were fishing.

I managed to photograph some of the central islands from the overcrowded Bissau to Bubaque ferry. The five hour sailing only cost £3. The seamost islands, which Drake must have seen, would have looked like all of the other islands.

Los Islands, Guinea Republic

Due to mutilation in *The Cotton Narrative*, we next hear of Hawkins anchored at a group of islands. On the swampy coast of present-day Guinea, the rivers are few. Hence, it was convenient to reassemble the fleet at the Los Islands, especially as they were so conspicuous by their height. These hilly, rocky, densely wooded islands, are in direct contrast to the flat shore. The two largest islands west to east are, Tamara and Kassa. They are both banana shape and face each other. They envelop a basin about a mile wide. Towards the south, but within the basin, is the third largest island. Three small islands form a curved chain between this island and Kassa, which gives the islands a distinct "U" shape. They lie between three and eight kilometres from the mainland Conakry peninsular. Shipping passes between Kassa and Conakry. No ships pass between the islands.

During a three day stay, Hawkins received a runaway Negro who had committed adultery with one of the King Zambulo's wives. He preferred to live in slavery than to face a cruel death. From Williamson's 1927 published studies [155] of *The Cotton Narrative*, he writes that this anchorage was at the Bijagos Islands. In his revised book of 1969, he suggests that it was at the Los Islands. Unwin subscribes to the former and states that Hawkins only watered at the Los Islands. Barrett only mentions one anchoring, after leaving the River Grande which was at the *Los Idolos* Islands. [Wright, 155] There is one clinching topographical clue in *The Cotton Narrative* which has been overlooked.

"Oure generall enquyred of him and if he cowld bring him where Sambulu was. He awnswered that he cowlde and poincted that his towne that he dwelled in was on the other side of a poincte of the mayne land, which we saw plainly where we road vnder one of the ilonds." [508]

The site of the town has been consumed by the capital city of Conakry. On the second visit, I secured views of this *poincte of the mayne land*. Conversely, to avoid running aground at the Bijagos islands, the closest Hawkins could have been to the shore was twenty five miles.

Hawkins must have anchored on the NE side of Kassa island, from where the Conakry peninsula is clearly seen. The men landed on the 100 metre long beach. The beach is dissected by a small and very shallow stream. From here, provisioning and watering parties were dispatched. On the NW side of Tamara is a fast flowing stream. It is not easily discernible because there are no beaches: only small rocks. My hired boatmen's intimate knowledge of the islands was vital because I did not notice the stream. It was a foot deep, two metres wide and flowed thirty metres from the undergrowth through a bowl-shaped channel. The stream was fed by a network of surface water, which gravitated into one channel just before it emerged from the foliage. I then realised that the fleet did not just collect this pure water, but could not have resisted the diverse fruits of the island's one big wild orchard. The sailors were meandering under a canopy of oranges, limes, bananas and coconuts.

There were bamboo trees, which were useful for long oars to hold a boat steady as the water barrels were loaded.

Due to the frequency of the white slavers, the islands were virtually uninhabited. Consequently, Hawkins followed the Negro ashore, only to find the relics of a cannibalism and human sacrifice. Meanwhile, he had sent the smaller vessels to the *Calousa* and *Casserroes* rivers, with orders to reunite at Sierra Leone. In the *Calousa*, Hortop vividly recalled how their small boat was overturned by a sea monster, which we would know as a hippopotamus. Before leaving the Los Islands, Hawkins had decided to visit the *Lengarrame* river to meet other boats, which he had dispatched. *The Cotton Narrative* does not indicate if this plan materialised.

It is impossible to positively identify these rivers, since these native names were phonetically recorded long before they were re-named on charts. Compared to what Drake saw on his voyages, these bland waterways continued to present the most boring landscapes.

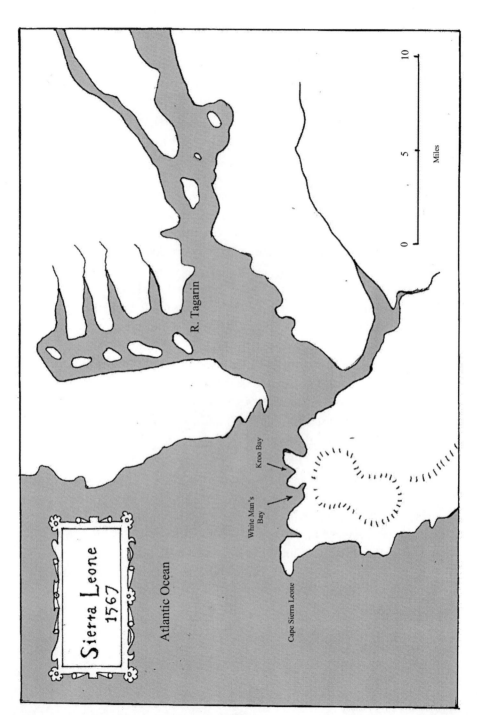

Sierra Leone
1567

Atlantic Ocean

R. Tagarin

White Man's
Bay

Kroo Bay

Cape Sierra Leone

0   5   10

Miles

Freetown, Sierra Leone

"...and sailed towardes Tagarring, otherwyse called Sierra Lion, where we arrived and came to anker 23rd of December,.."
[The Cotton Narrative, 509]

Upon initial study, this anchorage was an enigma because Sierra Leone is a country with several hundred miles of coastline. *The Famous Voyage* states that Sierra Leone was on the coast of Guinea. This implies that it was once a place and not a country. Sierra Leone was discovered by the Portuguese in the late 15th century. Its name means Lion Mountain Range because when it was discovered, thunder and lightning reverberated around the mountain peaks, giving rise to the notion that a lion lived within. The mountain range is a stunning landmark, since the entire West African coast is flat. The view upon arrival at the last of the great estuaries was: a flat shoreline to port and an eight mile wide waterway ahead, with mountains behind. However, due to the haze, the ships would have to be half way across the waterway before both banks could be discerned. On the mountain's north or estuary's south side, nestles Freetown, the capital of Sierra Leone. Its harbour is the best natural haven in West Africa. Its width ranges from eight to four miles wide. From where the English anchored, it was six miles to the north shore. Here, to the east of Tagarin Point, is the tributary estuary of the River Tagarin.

None of the accounts states exactly where the fleet anchored. However, Francis Pretty, who chronicled the Cavendish circumnavigation of 1586-88, used one of two adjacent bays, now known as **White Man's Bay** and Kroo Bay at Freetown. Pretty wrote that the ships were guided in to the haven by John Brewer, who was here with Drake in 1580. Drake had learnt of

the anchorage from the Lovell and Hawkins voyages. Pretty's description will be examined during Drake's 1580 sojourn.

The first two weeks were spent fishing, watering, wooding, provisioning and washing clothes. A river flows into both bays and many streams tumble into White Man's Bay. The densely wooded mountain slopes provide an infinite source of fruits. These blessings of nature impressed Hortop. Due to the absence of a camera or a shortage of artists, Hortop had to confine his communication to quaint words.

"The Plantan tree also groweth in that countrey; the tree is as bigge as a mans thigh, and as high as a firre pole, the leaves thereof be long and broard and on the top grow the fruit which are called Plantanos: they are crooked, and a cubite long; and as bigge as a mans wrist, they growe on clusters: when they be ripe they be very good and daintie to eate: Sugar is not more delicate in taste then they be." Hortop also saw, *"Sharkes,*

which will devoure men and...Palmito trees, which bee as high as a ships maine mast, and on their tops grow nuts," [op. cit. 337-9] I also found *monkeys,* but not the *muske-cats, which breed in hollow trees, trees...with Oisters upon them* and a *sea-horse* being a hippopotamus.

In an attempt to bolster the mere 150 slaves, Hawkins sent some of the smaller craft southward to the *Magrabomba* river. *The Cotton Narrative* does not say if the expedition yielded more than the futility of the *Calowsas* excursion. This river is probably the Number 1 River which lies half way down the Freetown Peninsula, since beyond this region, the number of major rivers diminish. The Freetown Peninsula seems to be the limits of Hawkins's river searches on this voyage. Furthermore, we have no idea if Drake went.

A native envoy invited Hawkins to participate in a local war and was to be given a share of the prisoners. Once again, African was fighting African: a situation which the White man never failed to exploit. Hawkins helped the King of Sierra Leone to capture the town of **Conga** on the **River Tagarin**, which was fortified by a circular wall of logs. The English attacked from the riverside, blasting gaps in the defences and burning the huts. The defendants were driven into the land-side mangrove swamps, where they were either drowned, slaughtered or seized by the Negro allies. Drowning awaited those who retreated into, *"...ye sea at low water, at the point of the land,.."* [Hortop, op. cit. 338] Hawkins had taken around fifty captives and was only given about 150. Out of the total captured his black cargo totalled between four to five hundred: sufficient for an Atlantic crossing. After more wooding and watering, the fleet of six English, two French and two Portuguese ships set sail in early February for Dominica.

Conga no longer exists and its exact location is beyond conjecture. *The Cotton Narrative* states that it *"was in the river of Tagarrin..."* [510] Since Hawkins was helping the King of Sierra Leone, the following statement which was written in 1564 during his second slaving voyage, suggests that Conga was on the north bank. *"...up the river...a great battell betweene them of Sierra Leona side, and them of Taggarin:"* [Hakluyt, Vol. VII. 19] A sketch map drawn in 1582 by Richard Maddox, during the Fenton voyage, shows the Tagarin flowing into the NE side of the bay. Like most places on the West African leg of this voyage, its importance is limited by the fact that we are not sure of Drake's exact whereabouts during the battle. Drake could have remained with the ships, which were most likely in White Man's Bay. To symbolise pictorially the episode, I photographed the whole harbour and hinterland from high up the mountain behind Freetown. In 1997 I photographed the harbour from the sea and tried to find Conga.

Just inside Cape Sierra Leone, at Man O' War Bay, I hired a boat for $20 an hour. The photography concentrated upon the coastline from the cape to White Man's Bay. The hills bordering the sea were visible but the Harmattan haze rendered a feint line of the distant mountain peaks. This matched the scene for Drake and Hawkins.

To sail behind Hawkins in search of Conga, I hired a boat adjacent to the Kissy Ferry Terminal and sailed to the far end of the Tagarin. Here we were boxed-in amid mangrove shallows. The river is home to a maze of islands; the largest being about 400 metres long. All support mangrove swamps and trees. On a few islands, firm land exists between the mangroves and supports small villages. I deduce that Conga stood on an island, about ten miles from White Man's Bay, near the west bank of

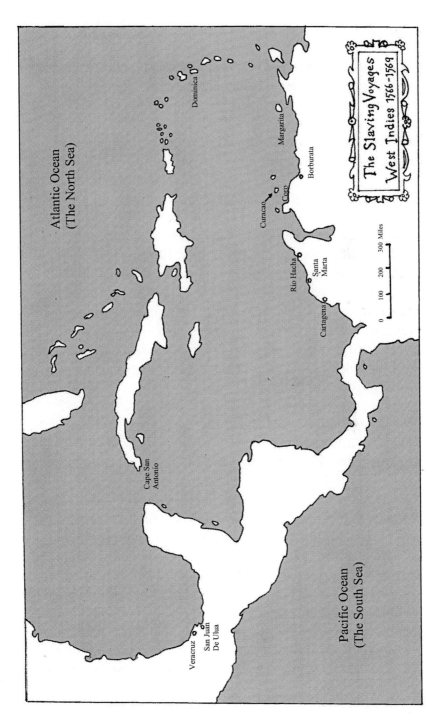

Atlantic Ocean
(The North Sea)

Dominica

Margarita

Borburata

Cape

Curacao

Rio Hacha

Santa
Marta

Cartagena

Cape San
Antonio

Veracruz
San Juan
De Ulua

Pacific Ocean
(The South Sea)

The Slaving Voyages
West Indies 1566-1569

0   100   200   300 Miles

47

the Tagarin. There are several possible sites. I photographed the two villages in this area and attained a visual glance of Hawkins's actions.

With a sufficient number of slaves to ensure an impressive profit, the fleet embarked upon an uneventful Atlantic crossing.

Douglas Bay, Dominica

Hawkins arrived here on 27 March 1568. This 27 by 12 mile lofty, rugged, mountainous island of volcanic origin, was discovered by Colombus on a Sunday, hence its name.

On the Lovell voyage there was no mention as to which island was used for provisioning. However, on all Hawkins's and Drake's Atlantic crossings, Dominica was usually sighted first. In 1564 Hawkins had used Dominica as his first anchorage. Hawkins then wrote,

"for we could finde none there but raine water, and such as fell from the hilles, and remained as a puddle in the dale."
[Hakluyt, Vol. VII. 20]

This suggests that Hawkins had encountered Douglas Bay on the island's NW shore, where sand bars still block the surface water from entering the sea. Only a narrow isthmus of land separated Hawkins from the island's best anchorage. All other anchorages on this lee side are open roadsteads. There are no suitable anchorages on the east coast as Colombus discovered in 1493. He had sent one of his caravels around to the sheltered side which reported dwellings in a huge bay. Here four streams and a river flow into the sea and from Job Hortop's account of Hawkins's 1568 sojourn, water did not seem to be a problem.

"...in sailing towards the Indies, the first land that we escryed, was the Iland called Dominica, where at our comming we anchored & tooke in fresh water and wood for our provision."
[Hakluyt, op. cit. 339]

The evidence so far for using the "huge bay" is circumstantial but William Parker who sailed on Drake's last voyage wrote during a subsequent voyage to the Caribbean, *"And if thou art going for Tierra firma, thou shalt goe West and by South untill thou come to Dominica, and there on the North west side is a river, where thou mayest water. The marks to know it bee a certaine high land full of hilles. And seeing it when thou art farre off to seaward, it maketh the middest a partition; so that a man would thinke it divided the Island in two parts."*
[Hakluyt, Vol. VII. 226]

I sympathised with this description when taking pictures from a low flying plane. In Drake's time, this anchorage was called the Great North West Bay. Today, it is Prince Rupert Bay and forms part of the Cabrits National Park.

According to Mr Lennox Honeychurch, a Dominican author of the island's history, who wrote the following for the Dominican Tourist Board, it is implied that the bay was well known to Drake's contemporaries.

"The name Cabrits comes from the Spanish, Portuguese and French word for goat because sailors left goats to run wild on the headland to secure fresh meat on future visits...After Colombus' second voyage in 1493 adventurers on ships of all nations used the bay to refresh their crews and trade with the Carib Indians for food after the long Atlantic crossing... Privateers and explorers, including Drake, Hawkins,..visited."

Although Job Hortop's brief description is the most detailed by comparison with either the Hawkins's or Philips's accounts, there is no mention of trade with the Caribs. However, during Drake's next visit, seventeen years later, truck with the natives was recorded and the evidence overwhelmingly suggests that Prince Rupert Bay was then used. Since this bay was discovered in 1493, and was vital for provisioning after transatlantic crossings, it must have been known to Drake in 1568. However, in 1564 Hawkins had anchored in the adjacent smaller bay to the north. The *West Indies Pilot* recommends ships to anchor about 1½ cables offshore, where the depth varies between 30 to 40 feet, over a sandy seabed.

Pampatar, Margarita Island, Venezuela

From the despatch of Licentiate Santiago de Riego to the Crown of May 12, 1567, [Wright, 17] we can infer that Captain John Lovell arrived during Easter 1567 with four ships. Lovell, appeared to have enjoyed amicable trading because the following year, Hawkins purchased more supplies and watered. Hawkins had arrived during the early evening. Immediately he sent a despatch to the Governor stating that he would be coming ashore at nine the following morning. Since only fifty Spaniards inhabited the island, their best form of defence was to extend the hand of cordiality. Hawkins was given a tour of the town and was banqueted during a stay of about nine days.

Due to being violently mugged, I arrived on Margarita in 1984 without a camera but armed with a letter of introduction from the British Embassy in Caracas. Consequently, to my good fortune, a shop lent me a camera for the week. I needed to examine three port towns because after three years of study, none of the accounts furnished any clues as to the whereabouts of the port in question. With the procuring of rare and specialist books, the research took more time than the field studies. It was not until 1988 that I read Job Hortop's recitation, which yielded the vital clue.

"A mile off the Iland there is a rocke in the sea, wherein doe breede many fowles like unto Barnacles: in the night we went out in our boates, and with cudgels we killed many of them and brought them with many of the egs aboord with us: their egges be as big as Turkies egges and speckled like them."
[Hakluyt, op. cit. 339]

Only off the port of Pampatar on the island's east shore is there a rock. It is nearly two miles seaward, about 150 metres long, thirty metres wide maximum and covered with pelicans. Their profusion would resemble that of barnacles. Due to a rough sea, I could not climb the rock by its rope and wood ladder to inspect any eggs.

I returned on Palm Sunday the following year. The sun shone and a calm sea enabled me to climb the ladder. As I did, the pelicans departed and encircled observing their invader. The view of the harbour from the top of the rock was excellent. Precariously, one can walk along the very narrow ridge for almost the entire length of the rock. In places on both sides, there is a near sheer drop of about twenty-five metres. The English, must have been very nimble on their feet as they clubbed the birds in the dark.

Disappointingly, there were no eggs: not even shells. I thought that if only the weather had been normal two Christmases ago, I would not have had to spend an extra £40 for partial advancement in covering this anchorage. The following January I returned for the last time. Again it was too rough for a landing. I was determined to quench my curiosity. It was 7am. I jumped into the surging sea and with great caution and timing, I scrambled up the wave-battered rock and ascended the ladder. There were no eggs! I had done my best for I would have to live here to find the eggs of a brown pelican. I was compensated in the sense that I was literally in the exact footsteps of Job Hortop and his shipmates, amongst whom could have been young Drake.

The town possesses one or two colonial houses. A fort which stands on the water front was under construction during Drake's visit. It was built to prevent the likes of the French from burning any more houses. Pampatar has always been the island's most important and only deep water port. Ships can anchor close inshore in the lee of the north point. Because the perennial NE Trades blow parallel to the town and the coast runs southwards, the English could have anchored half way between the town and the rock. This would enable the fleet to depart using the stiff breeze on a port beam reach. The south coast was skirted where the sails were trimmed for a broad starboard reach to *"Borboroata in the mayne land, a verry good port,.."* [Cotton, 515]

Borburata

Before leaving England, all I knew of its whereabouts, was from Corbett's description. He wrote that Borburata was a lonely port in the Gulf of Triste and from his study of the *Spanish López Atlas,* Madrid, 1736, it was four or five leagues east of present-day Puerto Cabello. I needed to narrow down the search. In the Caracas archives, there were 17th century maps of Borburata. They showed the cove to be only within two miles of Puerto Cabello, which has superseded this once important port. By walking along the beaches, remembering that in front of the cove was an island and that the cove lay obliquely to the coast, I was able to discover its true location and also realised how easy it would have been for Drake's contemporaries to find the sleepy haven. The island adjacent to the cove's mouth was the last of a chain of four, flat, small, green islets. Ships approaching from the east, would have passed them to port and rounded Isla del Rey, thus entering on a beam reach. Since the islands lay nearly a mile offshore, they formed a capacious sound, in which Hawkins anchored in deep, calm water in front of Borburata cove.

Both Lovell and Hawkins with their superior forces were able to careen their ships, sell some slaves, provision and water. Beaches line the arms of the cove and are strewn with little rocks. The bight consists of a fine sandy, gently shelving beach. Thirty-five metres out from the shore, was a row of plastic buoys. These marked a depth of four metres. One could clearly visualise, Hawkins's ships on the careen as the Black cargo was paraded ashore. The sea spills on to the beach and gently laps upon the cove's arms.

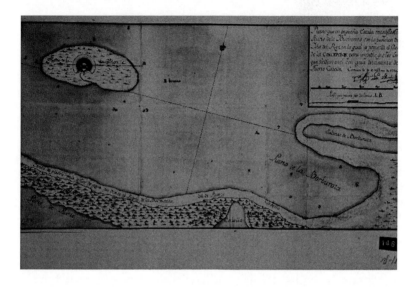

Today, the cove is naval property. On the west arm, there are petroleum storage tanks. Beach bungalows occupied by service personnel line the east shore. Because all modern fixtures are set in from the cove, the photographic potential was pleasing. On the first visit, I had innocently entered the cove from the beach at its NE point and left via the main gate where I was quietly rebuked. During the re-visit, I departed along the coast. The third visit was on a hot, sunny, December day. Again, I entered from the beach. After I had taken all the pictures, I was discovered by a young security guard who escorted me to the gate. Sometimes trying to obtain permission is too time consuming for a very short trip and is not guaranteed. If I were refused and later caught trespassing, the consequences could be unpleasant. On some occasions, I keep a low profile pleading

ignorance and just risk expulsion with a camera full of
undeclared exposures.

During Hawkins's eight week stay from Easter Eve of the 17
April until the beginning of June, much time was spent waiting
for replies to applications for a licence to sell slaves, from the
officials who lived inland. His applications were met with
refusals which echoed the King's orders. Hawkins had
unofficially sold some Negroes to the coastal dwellers, from
whom he was encouraged to send a contingent of men up to the
inland town of Valencia to physically force its merchants to
trade. The merchants who tacitly desired to trade could then
defend themselves against any official or royal rebuke.
However, the town was found abandoned. Since Drake was a
senior mariner, it is unlikely that he went. The present road to
Valencia is dual carriageway and carpets a valley. Valencia is a
sprawling city that nestles in the hills. No pictures could be
taken to remotely resemble what the party may have seen.

The main reason for my third visit in 1998, was to document Drake's approach, anchoring and departure. This "Drake port" fronted by islets and backed by the domineering and majestic Andes mountains, gave Borbuarata a unique geographical setting. Due to the coast being back-lit, I had to hire the boat from Puerto Cabello early in the morning and late in the afternoon to achieve side-lit exposures. These excursions totalled an expensive $75.

Coro

The following extract from *The Cotton Narrative*, enhances the probability that Drake did not go to Valencia.

"Thus having bene here above a monethe, oure generall, before he wold depart with all the ships from hence, sente certaine of them awaye to Coresau, an ilond which lieth in the sea in the waye that we showlde goe, there to provyde beef and motton whereof there is greate plenty in the ilond, and to drye it to serve vs for victuals homeward. Alsoe he sente ij barkes to a place named Coro, not farre from Borborata, to se what good there mighte be done there in selling of wares." [519]

It is pretty clear that Hawkins arrived at Borburata with nine ships, six of his own and three Frenchmen. He specifically dispatched the barks, identified as the fifty ton *Judith*, commanded by Drake, and the *Angel* to trade at Coro. Nothing is known of the excursion because of mutilation in *The Cotton Narrative*. However, from a letter written by Diego Ruiz de Vallejo, Accountant, on 21 April, 1568 [Wright, 114] that refers to the Lovell visit, would indicate that no trade was conducted at Coro during both voyages.

"These two (Bontemps and the Englishman) came to a mutual understanding and treated for peace with the people and promised to give one hundred slaves to the royal treasury if they were permitted to sell two hundred more and their other merchandise. To this effect they sent from Borburata to the port of El Coro a request that the governor might grant them the license, but the said governor refused it and ordered that no trading be done."

Most likely, Hawkins sent Drake because he had been to Coro the year before. This port would have been easy to find. As the barks skirted the shore, their westward passage would have been blocked by a wall of land protruding fifty miles to the north. Immediately before this peninsula, was the port for Coro called La Vela de Coro, or in English, The Candle of Coro. The "candle" is the peninsula and forms the west shore of the bay, about twenty miles along which, the land fans out to the west. On a map, it gives the image of a candle flame being blown westwards by the NE Trades.

Drake would have anchored about a mile towards the NE - any closer would have risked running aground in the shallow bay, or being blown on to the Candle which is noted for its huge sand dunes. Since the eastern promontory of the bay affords only modest protection from the stiff trades, the present-day port village has hardly expanded beyond its 16th century dimensions. Coro has remained seven miles SW inland from its port. The city was founded in 1527, being the oldest in Venezuela and the country's first capital.

To establish contact with a boat owner, I had to swim out to a mooring. The hire price was only £3, probably because the inhabitants had little truck with foreigners. Pictures depicted Drake's approach and scenes from the anchorage. In case he landed, a view from the village's easterly point provided a sweeping view along the beach to the beginning of the Candle peninsula. Despite Coro only having a tenuous connection with Drake, its inclusion has left nothing to chance.

Curaçao

However, the fleet did unite somewhere at the thirty mile long island of Curaçao. Therefore I had to find the most likely anchorage by process of elimination. This involved inspecting the entire island by air and sea. Most of the island's anchorages are on the south indented shore, all of which are well protected from the NE Trades that beat the north coast. The few harbours are described from east to west.

The *South America Pilot Vol. 4*, states that Caracas Bay is too deep for anchoring.

Halfway along the island, is the visually stunning, four mile long, open Bullen Bay. This is the largest and deepest haven, which again, enables oil tankers to anchor at the refinery towards its NW end. It is well sheltered by hills rising from its head. The *South American Pilot* again states that, "depths are too great for anchoring."

The small idyllic coves of Santa Cruz and Playa Jeremi are too small to house a fleet of nine ships and would have been ignored. Westpunt Bay at the island's far end possesses two landing beaches and ships can anchor close inshore, but the depths are "considerable." [ibid]

My interest and conclusions, eventually focused upon two small graffiti-covered forts. This virtually proves that, sailing ships were anchored under the protection of the forts' guns. The forts dominate a 200 metre long beach, over the bight or, open **Bay of St Michiel,** two miles east of Bullen Bay. The *South American Pilot* states that, this sheltered bay affords a good and safe anchorage in a depth of forty metres, one cable offshore. However, depths can be more considerable.

To establish that this was the most probable landing site, I hired a boat to skirt the bay in search for other landing beaches. Only at the far NW end could a landing be effected. Here, the cliff-faced plateau is punctuated by an uninviting platform of broken coral. As I returned and stepped ashore at St. Michiel, I felt sure that Drake had done the same. I was reassured when I looked up at the forts which testify to the port's strategic past.

Rio Hacha, Colombia

Nuestra Señora de los Remedios del Rio Hacha was founded by Nicolás Federmann in 1545. By 1568 it was a settlement of about eighty souls, living in sixty mud and thatched huts. The church and the treasurer's house were the only substantial buildings. Consequently, nothing of 16th century Rio Hacha remains. Ships had to anchor in the open roadstead. The blue sea suddenly becomes brown within of a quarter of a mile of the beach because of the muddy Rio Hacha, which today is called the Rancheria. Like Margarita, it was famous beyond its size for its pearls.

At Curaçao, Hawkins sent the *Angel* and Drake in the *Judith*, ahead to Rio Hacha. The treasurer, Miguel Castellanos had refused to trade with the Lovell expedition. Consequently,

Lovell remained anchored in the open roadstead for a week trying to force trade but left empty-handed despite landing ninety-two Negroes. The Spanish sources report that shots were exchanged and Lovell was prevented from landing. The depositing of slaves under the cover of darkness was Lovell's last desperate act.

"...an hour after nightfall, the English set ashore ninety-two pieces of blacks, all old, and very sick and thin. Nobody could prevent their doing this because they landed them on the other side of the river, in a place to which none could cross from the city because the river was very high at the time." [Clerks of the council, Wright, 106] *"The night before he left, it being dark, he set ashore ninety-six of the oldest, thinnest slaves he had, because they were dying on his hands. Because he set them ashore at a point somewhat distant from the town, on the other side of a large river, we were not aware of it until he had landed them and was returning to his ships. He made sail and went up the coast until he crossed to Española, where we know that he did very great damage."*
[Hernándo Costilla & Lazaro de Vallejo Aldrete, Wright, 110]

Lovell's next documented anchoring was back in Plymouth.

From the English point of view, Lovell had been tricked into landing human cargo for remuneration that was not forthcoming. Conversely, one can perceive that like Hawkins, Lovell adopted a high-handed approach to coerce the struggling colonists to buy slaves. Drake who was now off the town, with this episode fresh in his mind, was eager to redress the balance sheet and take the upper hand. The request for water was met with gunfire. Drake reciprocated and damaged the treasurer's house. The two ships withdrew from range and blockaded the port for five days. During which time, Drake ransacked an unsuspecting despatch vessel arriving from Santo Domingo.

Hawkins appeared on the 10 June. That night, he sent a letter ashore. As usual, it was to the point: that the sale of sixty Negroes was required to help defray the costs of the voyage. The letter contained a thinly disguised threat of force. Furthermore, as a sweetener, Hawkins was prepared to overlook last year's incident, blaming Lovell for a degree of incompetence. Despite the ten menacing sails, the treasurer was defiant. His confidence, was still riding high from sending Lovell away empty-handed.

The Cotton Narrative mentions that Hawkins landed with 200 men at sunrise, which would be at 6 am. The Spanish sources claim at noon. [Wright, 116-123] The Lazario and Castellanos accounts state the landing was between half and three quarters of a league away respectively. After the English had marched a quarter of a mile, they encountered a barricade blocking the road. This would suggest that the landing was effected to the west of Rio Hacha because the deep river, coupled with a barricade, would have made a very strong defence. Furthermore, we learn from the Spanish accounts of the Lovell landing, that there was no bridge across the river. The defendants at the blockade fled into the *"woodes"* when the ships fired their cannons, allowing Hawkins to occupy a deserted town.

In fact, the surrounding countryside is of sand supporting three metre high trees with small drought resistant leaves, interspersed with cactus. The coastal road into the town, is over a rocky plateau two metres above the endless beach. Two cannons had been brought ashore and trained inland. Curiously,

The Cotton Narrative states that the inhabitants were warned not to appear over the hill. There is no hill. The land is flat.

Hawkins threatened to burn the town unless he was granted a licence. Due to a break down in communication within the English ranks, some houses were burnt by mistake. The citizens who were now living in the bush, wanted to trade on Hawkins's fair terms. Castellanos remained steadfast to the royal line. Meanwhile, a runaway Negro entered the English lines and in return for freedom, led Hawkins six miles inland to a tent where all the treasure was hidden. Two carts loaded the pearls, gold and silver for safe storage in the town. Castellanos under immense pressure, agreed to *"mette alone together in a faire plaine..."* [Cotton, 525] This would have been one of the many clearings which still exist several miles inland. Hawkins had to hand over the Negro and a mulatto who had also deserted. They were quartered and hanged respectively.

After two weeks, over 200 slaves were either sold or given as compensation for the destroyed property. Rio Hacha proved to be the most lucrative port of call. By now, most of the slaves were sold. During these transactions, the seamen had to amuse themselves elsewhere. Hortop and six others rowed up the forty metre wide river, towing a dog which was tied to a meat hook. It had the desired effect. A crocodile became hooked as it ate the dog. The beast was stuffed and shipped aboard the fleet, which sailed according to *The Cotton Narrative*, on 1 July for Santa Marta.

Santa Marta

This town was the oldest established on the mainland. It had been founded by Rodrigo de Batidas in 1525. *A relation of the ports, harbors, forts and cities in the west indies by Baptista Antonio 1587*, [Hakluyt, Vol. VII. 109] gives us a good description of the harbour.

"...the city being situated upon a sandy bay adjoyning unto the sea side, conteineth in it about 30. housholds; all the houses being made of canes, and covered over with Palmito trees, and some of them be covered with tyle...They have traffike with none, but with the Indians...It is a countrey which hath but small store of cattel, because it is all mountainous,... There is a very good harbour before the said towne, invironed with mighty hils & great rocks, which reach even unto the sea side, the which hie land doth greatly succour the harbour, as also two Ilands which lie about three quarter of a league on the North side: so that although they be subject to Easterly winds, and that with the great stormes, yet they doe no greate harme to goe on land."

Due to Santa Marta never being fortified to prevent its regular sacking and its limited trading status, only a few buildings survive from its early colonial past. However, the geographical descriptions remain ever apparent. The Indian population is now concentrated in the Sierra Madre, which form a dominating backdrop and cattle wander the flat coastal plain.

The panoramic view over the bay from the north headland was of great interest but the picture was obtained at a high cost. I was returning to the town, when on the edge of a shanty town, a tall black man spoke to me. I did not understand him and was a little suspicious. I walked on and then was strangled from behind. As he slashed the back of my ear, his accomplice took my feet away from underneath me. The switch-blade was used to chisel off my watch. In fear of my life, I released the camera bag. The accomplice ran off with the valuables as the other thief walked away with the knife in his hand. I confronted the witnesses with the police but they were too frightened to admit to have seen anything. I could only rely upon the travel insurance for effective compensation. After eighteen months of anxiety, I returned for the lost picture. I was lucky. I had hitched a ride on a lorry to Santa Marta, on top of which I met César Riascos. This burly Colombian, spent much of his spare time promoting the living conditions of the Cogi Indians who inhabit the Sierra Madre. He gave up more of his time to be my bodyguard. For extra security, I hired a taxi, which managed to traverse the rough terrain to the headland. On a subsequent visit to Colombia, César was to help me with boat hire. His hospitality and the eventual successful documentation, presented a more balanced experience in this potentially dangerous part of the world.

Hawkins arrived on the 10 July. If the dates are correct, the sailing was painfully slow. For Hawkins and Drake, this was the furthest they had sailed along the mainland coast. The previous voyages had swung north from Rio Hacha, to Española. Hawkins must have calculated that he may be more welcome at a fresh port, in which to off-load the remaining 150 Negroes. Soon after arrival in the evening, a letter was sent ashore. A receptive reply was immediately dispatched. As agreed, Hawkins landed at 10 am next morning and discussed a face-saving plan in which to receive a licence. Hawkins returned to his ships and assembled 150 men which were ferried ashore. Simultaneously, the ships fired at the town, destroying a pre-determined house. Hawkins then occupied the main square and was met by a flag of truce. Over the next two weeks, 110 Negroes were sold and fresh fruit, beef and water were shipped aboard. Hawkins departed 26 July hoping that the remaining forty slaves could be sold at Cartagena.

Cartagena

Cartagena was the jewel in the Spanish colonial crown. The town was almost an island. The shallow sea made it obligatory to approach the town from a near land-locked lagoon which formed the most capacious harbour in Spanish America. Ships usually entered through the 1,400 yard wide Boca Grande two miles south of the town. Five miles further south, was the 900 yard entrance of Boca Chica or "little mouth."

Hawkins realised that this rich and well defended town of 500 soldiers, with strong native support, could not be amicably bullied into buying slaves. His letter to purchase just provisions was begrudgingly opened by the governor, who refused to supply even water. From the inner harbour, Hawkins initiated the futile exchange of artillery. Meanwhile, his pinnaces had reported water and orchards on the island of **Tierra Bomba,** which forms the south shore of the main entrance to the outer harbour. Hawkins gladly exploited these blessings of nature. Contrary winds extended the stay to about seven days. During this time, Drake had carefully studied Cartagena's strengths, weaknesses and surrounding geography, which he was later to use to a devastating effect. Outside the haven, probably in sight of Islas del Rosario, the fleet was becalmed for two days. One of the French ships was discharged and the now ramshackle bark purchased at the *Rio Grande* was scuttled.

Tierra Bomba is reached by taking the local shuttle boat. The same well is now the focal point of a village! This far west along the Caribbean coast, the vegetation is lush, so the island is densely wooded. From my observations, there were no orchards and the trees grew wild. The Rosario Islands can be visited by daily tour boats from Cartagena. They are a string of tiny, flat, islets, ringed with white sand and coral, upon which grow palm trees.

The hurricane season was imminent so with fifty-seven unsold slaves and £13,500 in gold silver and pearls aboard, Hawkins cut his losses and steered for the Florida Channel to exit the Caribbean.

Cape San Antonio, Cuba

"Thus we sayled, directing oure cowrse with Cabo Sainct Anton of the Ilond of Cuba, meaning nowe to staye no where but to desemboke the channell of Bahama..." [Cotton, 530] *" From Cartagena they made sail for Cape San Anton in order to disembogue and were delayed by contrary weather in doubling that cape."* [Barrett, Wright, op. cit. 158]

The cape was famous because it was a convenient haven for shipping plying between México and Cuba. Due to the cape's isolation, sailors could refresh themselves and air their ships unmolested. Drake most likely saw this cape in passing and recognised its value, which he was later to exploit. The best contemporary description of the cape, is furnished by an unnamed seaman on Drake's last voyage. *"Cape S. Antonio,.. being a low cape...and to the Southwest a white sandie bay where 3 or 4 ships may very well water. There is a good road for North & Easterly windes: .."*
[Anonymous Text, Hakluyt, Vol. VII. 198]

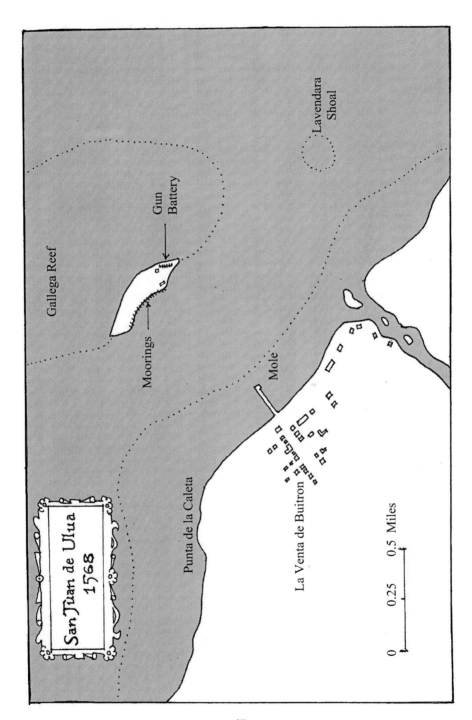

San Juan de Ulua
1568

Gallega Reef

Gun Battery

Moorings

Lavendara Shoal

Mole

Punta de la Caleta

La Venta de Buitron

0   0.25   0.5 Miles

The low, sandy cape curves so gently, over seven miles, that there is no bay. However, this SW shoreline would be the most protected stretch from the prevailing NE Trades.

Straits of Florida

On 12 August between Florida and Cuba a tempest was encountered. The *William and John* became separated but made it home. Largely on account of the *Jesus* splitting at her seams, the seven ships were helplessly blown bare poles westward. Hawkins had to seek a Spanish-held port for repairs. A passing Spanish vessel informed him that the nearest haven was San Juan de Ulua in México.

Veracruz, México

It was a dire emergency that had caused an English fleet to penetrate this far west. The Spaniards mistook the arrival of Hawkins for the annual flotilla. Sailing out from San Juan de Ulua to meet the fleet, included the treasurer and deputy governor. This delegation saw storm battered sails, and did not notice the faded flags of St. George and the lions and lucis. Hawkins reassured the dispirited reception committee with his requirement for the briefest stay to administer repairs and to purchase victuals. Due to Hawkins's potential strength, the Spaniards had to comply. Next day the 16 September, Hawkins entered the harbour and anchored alongside eight Spanish ships.

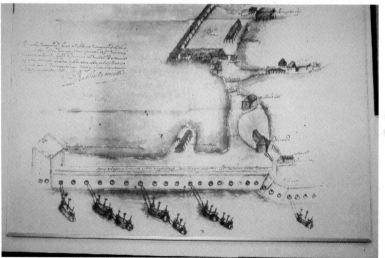

The port for Veracruz was formed by a 200 yard long fortified island, being 400 yards off shore. The island possessed a chapel, huts and a battery, which helped buffet the anchorage from the stiff rain-laden northerlies, which I experienced when documenting the port at the same time of year. The island is now joined to the mainland town of Veracruz by a dock complex. In Drake's day, Veracruz was situated eighteen miles to the NW. From Hawkins we are given a graphic description of the port, the topography of which has hardly altered.

"Now it is to be understood that this port is made by a little Iland of stones not three foote above the water in the highest place, and but a bow shoot of length any way, this Iland standeth from the maine land two bow shootes or more, also it is to be understood that there is not in all this coast any other place for ships to arrive in safety, because the North winde hath there such violence, that unlesse the shippes be very safely mored with their ankers fastened upon this Iland, there is no remedie for these North windes but death also the place of the Haven was so little, that of necessitie the shippes must ride one aboord the other,.." [Hakluyt, op. cit. 57]

All ships had their prows secured over the island, whilst stern anchors prevented ships swinging into collision. On average, twenty- five feet separated these larger ships, whilst the smaller ones anchored out in the harbour.

An air of uneasiness pervaded throughout the port as the annual flotilla was expected daily. Hawkins had already incurred the queen's wrath over his armed reaction to a Spanish fleet which had undignifiedly entered the Cattewater at the outset of the voyage. Hawkins now had to think of a harmonious plan of coexistence. If the Spanish fleet was denied entry, it would have been wrecked and for Hawkins, the diplomatic ramifications would be ruinous.

The next morning being Friday, seventeen sails were observed to seaward. Francis de Luxan commanded the flotilla which was carrying the incoming Viceroy of New Spain. Antonio Delgadillo, Captain and Inspector of the island and port of San

Juan de Ulua, greeted Don Martin Enríquez, with the disturbing news that heretic interlopers were illegally occupying the port. Furthermore, to the rage of the most distinguished aristocratic, royal emissary, this piratical English sea captain had dictated terms of entry to his own port. The English were to man the island and there was to be an exchange of gentlemen hostages. Beneath his smiling veneer, Enríquez had no intention to acquiesce. His hostages were common seamen. Enríquez took the view that there was no deceit when honour needed to be avenged against the likes of Hawkins who had no right to strike deals. The agreements were finalised on the Saturday but bad weather prevented entry until Tuesday 21st.

The fleets anchored side-by-side and an eerie peace ensued. During this period, Enríquez ordered soldiers to be slipped aboard an empty hulk. Hawkins who suspected treachery by the movement of men, twice sent Robert Barrett to the Viceroy to voice concern. An hour before the battle erupted, he was thrown into the hold of the Spanish flagship, and began many years in captivity. The Spaniards ejected the English from the gun emplacements and Hawkins now came under the fire from his own cannons. The island battery sank the *Angel*, drove men out of the *Swallow* and crippled the *Jesus*. However, from the sinking flagship, the treasure was rescued: three quarters of which was in gold. As the £10,000 in gold weighed about 225 pounds; it gives us a degree of the amount of labour involved under battle conditions. Drake's ship the *Judith*, and the *Minion* were too small to be of fighting worth, and withdrew out of range. Drake made off that night of 23 September and docked in Plymouth on 20 January 1569.

In 1980, I had visited San Juan de Ulua fortress purely as a sightseeing traveller. By sheer coincidence, in the fort's museum I saw Drake's portrait and from previous reading, vaguely remembered the story. A week later I became bored, and realised that to justify continued world travel, would require a main objective. I had been excited to stand on the same piece of ground as my school boy hero and decided to photograph Drake's world. This would give me incentive to continue learning Spanish, provide my travels with a sense of purpose and enable me to achieve something different for which, I would become noted. Therefore this experience would change the rest of my life! It was here that the *In Drake's Wake* project was born.

During the second visit to the fort it was being renovated. The museum was closed. After coming all this way, I could not accept being denied a photograph of the 16th century print depicting the fortified anchorage. I leant against a door which conveniently opened. The black and white drawing compares favourably with what can be seen today. For example, even the rings affixed to the fort's walls, through which passed the ships' hawsers, still match the sketch. Unfortunately, this fortified wall was superimposed upon the water front as a consequence of the battle of San Juan de Ulua, and not completed until the 1590s. A plaque bluntly describes Drake and Hawkins as pirates.

Plymouth to London

William Hawkins and Drake rode to London with letters for the government describing the outcome of the voyage. It was Drake's experience at San Juan de Ulua which fuelled his personality to send his career on to a higher plane.

Hawkins in the *Minion* reached Mount's Bay in Cornwall on 25 January. Only seventy men had returned in two ships. In his first account of the voyage, presented to the privy council, Hawkins wrote that the *Judith*, "forsooke us in our great miserie:.." [Hakluyt, Vol. VII. 60] Such sharpened language was used to highlight Hawkins's desire to seek redress. In his second account he simply wrote, "the bark Judith lost us." During the battle of San Juan de Ulua only about seventy English perished. The real "miserie" took hold after the battle because there was insufficient food aboard Hawkins's ship for the homeward voyage. Men had to be marooned on the Mexican coast! Although later in life, Drake's jealous enemies reminded him of his quasi-desertion, Hawkins seemed to have overlooked this incident, as he never made any other public statement. This was partly because he gave no formal instructions to his novice captain. Drake must have explained to Hawkins that he was on a lee shore, surrounded by reefs and shoals and in the teeth of a hurricane force wind.

Hawkins would continue to employ Drake. John Hawkins's elder brother William, and Drake were personal friends. William's son was to sail on Drake's world voyage. Hawkins and Drake became long-standing business partners and often underwrote each other's property deals. Some of Drake's Plymouth properties were direct purchases from the Hawkins family. Finally both men always appeared to cooperate with each other, in their joint efforts to serve the realm. They were both destined for knighthoods

Chapter Three

1569-1570:Home Waters &
The Married Merchant

La Rochelle, France, or Hamburg, Germany

For 1569, we have no proof of Drake's nautical movements:
only speculation. Lady Eliott-Drake wrote that during the early
part of 1569, Drake sailed with Sir William Winter to the relief
of La Rochelle. She does not cite her source. Thomson has
reproduced this claim, defining the relief as supplies and arms.
However, the great Victorian Drake biographer and naval
historian, Sir Julian Corbett surmises that a seaman as
experienced as Drake, would have volunteered or been pressed
into serving under Sir William Wynter, master of Naval
Ordnance and Surveyor of Ships. Furthermore, Drake would
have been eager to manifest his patriotic naval loyalties, after
the rift with Hawkins at San Juan de Ulua.

In the Thames, two fleets of merchantmen were awaiting
convoy. The wine fleet was bound for La Rochelle, to be
commanded by Sir John Basing. La Rochelle was a port
controlled by French Protestant Huguenots in their struggle
against the ruling Catholics. The wool flotilla with a guard of
seven warships, was destined for Hamburg, which was also
held by Protestants in their religious struggle against the
Spaniards, who occupied the Low Countries. Both fleets sailed
in April on a mission, blending commerce with support of their
rebellious, religious allies. Action was expected near or at
Hamburg from the Spaniards. Hence, this is one of the two
reasons why Corbett places Drake as a master in this fleet.

Rochester, Kent

This fleet returned to Rochester in early June from an uneventful excursion. The La Rochelle flotilla returned in July. Returning from the former crossing would have given Drake time to arrange his wedding.

Saltash, Cornwall

Edmund's sister Anna married William Barrett of Saltash. Their son was Robert Barrett and was Drake's cousin. Robert was Hawkins's flag-captain in the *Jesus* and was burned at the stake in Seville. A Harry Newman also served on this 1567-8 voyage. Drake married Mary Newman on 4 July 1569. According to the Tamar Protection Society, she was born in 1552 and was the daughter of Richard Newman. Her cottage is supposed to be in Culver Lane, Saltash. The existing 15th century cottage has recently been restored by the Society, which states that the cottage is a rare example of a small mediaeval house, retaining its original atmosphere. It has a central passage and two pole staircases leading to two rooms. However, since Mary was married in St Budeaux Church, it is most likely that she hailed from Saltash Passage on the Devon side of the Tamar. The visit to the cottage served to document completely Mary Newman's home because it was from the long garden of the cottage, which best rendered an elevated view of Saltash Passage!

St Budeaux, Devon

St Budeaux Church was the first Plymouth post Reformation church. Its high altar dates from 1563. As I stood just before the altar step, I must have been standing exactly where Drake took his vows. In 1560 Mary Newman's eldest sister Margaret, married John Bodenham at St Budeaux Church. From 1581, their son Jonas, became Drake's personal assistant, whom Drake treated like a son.

Plymouth

From Sugden and the West Devon Record Office, we learn that in 1570, Drake and his wife settled in Plymouth. Susan Jackson has studied one of Drake's leases that is housed in *The Plymouth Black Book*. Dame Margery, Drake's grandmother, left him property in Looe Street. It is possible that Drake lodged here when he returned from Kent and where he began married life. It was a contemporary custom for the wife, to live initially with the husband's family. This would have made sense because Mary was only about eighteen. She would have appreciated female family company during her husband's periods of absence.

A deed dated 1576 confirms that Drake held land known as Duberon's Chantry, located on the north side of Notte Street. The property possibly comprised a tenement and a garden. This property is again mentioned as belonging to Drake when he left on his world voyage. However, there is no proof that Drake was actually living here.

Public Works

Drake's name appears on a list of freemen who enjoyed the right to trade. By law, all merchants of substance, paid a commensurate rate, that funded such projects as: harbour and fortification improvements. By 1572-3 Drake would have been well placed to afford generous donations.

A 1572 entry in *The Plymouth Black Book* by Mayor John Blythman reads: *"Mo thatt this yere the kaye on the southesyde whereof the southe ende adjoneth to the Barbygan vnderneth the Castell was Builded by the towne vnder full sea marcke and contayneth in lengthe one hundred and Thurtie Foot and in Bredethe fourtie and fower foot."*

The 1576 deed states that Drake was a merchant. This year, Drake and Hawkins chartered out a vessel each, to a foreign merchant living in London. Therefore it is not surprising to learn that in 1576, Drake contributed 40 shillings towards the construction of the New Quay. The quayside was extended on the west side of Sutton Pool, between Southside Street and the Mayflower Steps.

By standing with your back towards the harbour and facing Southside Street, you can see two lines of cobbles, which nowadays, marks the width of the road. The closer line marks the extent of the Tudor extension. More extension lines can be seen at the edge of Vauxhall Street; since the road is on the site of the old quay.

Chapter Four

The Caribbean Voyages of 1570 & 1571

Sources

The English accounts of these voyages were compiled by Drake's preacher, Philip Nicholls, who had sailed with Drake on the later West Indies and Cádiz ventures. This material had been compiled into a book called *Sir Frances Drake Revived.* The introduction states that Drake edited the text. He presented the manuscript to the queen as a New Year's gift on 1 January 1593. Its aim was to illuminate his glorious past, during his period of maritime inactivity and to persuade Elizabeth to send him on another voyage, which transpired to be his last. The material has largely been substantiated by the Spanish documents but does suffer from some exaggerations. *Drake Revived* was eventually published by Drake's nephew in 1626. The Spanish accounts are found in, *Documents Concerning English Voyages To The Spanish Main*, by Irene A. Wright, who has also reprinted *Drake Revived.*

Outline of the first two voyages

In 1570 and 1571 Captain Francis Drake made reconnaissance voyages to Panamá in order to learn of the movements of shipping and treasure and with the purpose of burying stores in preparation for his famous plundering voyage of 1572-3. The queen found no recompense from the king of Spain for losses sustained by her and those concerned at the battle of San Juan de Ulua. Drake used this outcome and, to stretch the point, the conflicts at Rio Hacha to bend his career towards one of financial revenge. His crusade to chip away at the edges of the ever expanding and threatening evils of the Catholic empire was to be coloured by the banners of patriotism and Protestantism. Hence within a year of San Juan de Ulua, he was innovatively exploring the weak link of Spain's treasure chain between the House of Trade in Seville and the mines of South America. This was in Panamá . Here the treasure was debarked at Panama City and conveyed fifty miles across the mountainous isthmus by mules to the Atlantic port of Nombre de Dios for shipment to Spain.

From *Drake Revived*, which thoroughly documents his third voyage to Panamá, we learn that in 1570 Drake sailed with the *Dragon* and the 25 ton *Swan*. Research by Kelsey suggests that Drake set sail in the *Brave* on 25 November 1569 carrying goods to Guinea. Hawkins then returned home, despatching Drake to the Indies with two other ships. Drake was to become the first Englishman to raid the Caribbean. There is an absence of complaint from the Spanish sources, which indicates that the voyage was mainly one of reconnaissance. Drake had gained important knowledge about the shipping routes, the conveyance of merchandise along the River Chagres and intimate knowledge of the most secluded havens. The latter would serve as his supply lines and lairs, from where he could attack unsuspecting shipping. The intelligence gathered, along with potential plunder, animated Drake's backers to subscribe to a more ambitious expedition.

On the second voyage the *Swan* was his only ship. It is speculated that the Hawkins family were Drake's backers. This is because on the third voyage Drake also took the *Pasco*, also spelt as *Pasha,* which in two lists was stated as forty and eighty

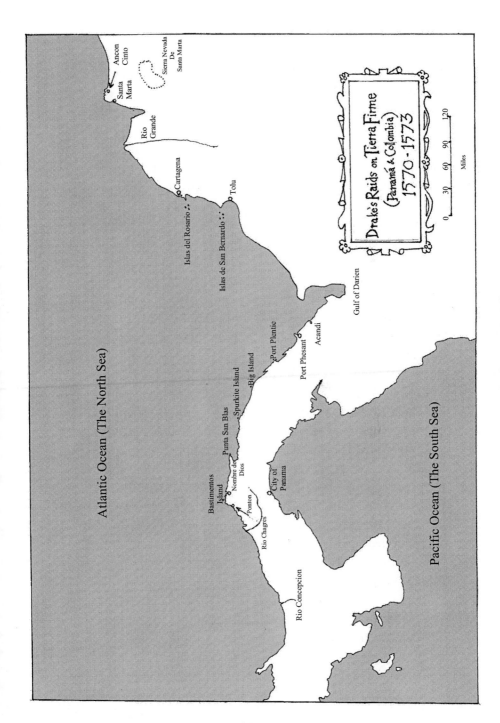

Atlantic Ocean (The North Sea)

Pacific Ocean (The South Sea)

Ancon Cinto

Sierra Nevada De Santa Marta

Santa Marta

Rio Grande

Cartagena

Tolu

Islas del Rosario

Islas de San Bernardo

Gulf of Darien

Acandi

Port Plentie

Port Phesant

Big Island

Spurkite Island

Punta San Blas

Bastimentos Island

Nombre de Dios

Ponton

City of Panama

Rio Chagres

Rio Concepcion

Drake's Raids on Tierra Firme
(Panamá & Colombia)
1570 - 1573

Miles

0   30   60   90   120

81

tons and belonged to the Hawkins. This variation in tonnage was not unusual. Alternatively, from the high profits obtained from the 1571 voyage, Drake may have purchased the *Pasco*.

Drake Revived barely provides a scant outline of the 1571 voyage. It is only from the Spanish accounts of the robberies committed by the English that we can partially reconstruct Drake's movements. Based upon the practice of all transatlantic voyages upon entering the Caribbean water and fruits would have been taken at Dominica or on a neighbouring island.

San Blas Islands

East of Nombre de Dios, the islands and the coastline were uninhabited. Therefore upon reaching Panamá by February 1571 Drake would have established a clandestine base amongst these 360 islets and small islands. They lie immediately east of Point San Blas and extend 100 miles. In Drake's time the point and islands were called the Cativas. During the nineteenth century, when the Cuna Indians settled the islands, the forest cover was stripped for a coco-palm economy. To see so many islands in such a small area was to be one of Drake's unique geographical experiences. The closer Drake sailed to Point San Blas the more numerous the islands became. If the past can be judged by the present, the configuration of the islands were identical in appearance. From here Drake sailed westward.

Puerto "Pontón" to Naranjo Keys

This is the first Spanish record of where the English asserted their presence. During the afternoon of Wednesday 21 February 1571, a Spanish frigate intending to enter Nombre de Dios was blown past it and anchored fourteen leagues to westward, at what Wright has translated as the Pontoon. This suggests that there was a wooden jetty within a bay. According to Doña Juana de Estrada and Luis de Soto, whilst at anchor, they were attacked by a pinnace. They prevented the "pirates" from boarding their higher sided vessel. As another frigate was passing by, the attackers set off to capture it. Meanwhile, the surviving crew cut their cable and drifted towards a mangrove islet, to which they waded. Here they watched the returning freebooters plunder their frigate. The English left an unsigned letter in the frigate, that referred to a skirmish a few days earlier, when no Spaniard was hurt. The letter explained that if the vessel had surrendered under a flag of truce no lives would have been endangered. This is the first record we have of Drake establishing his code of conduct: to minimise the casualties of battle. This was to be his lifelong stamp, from which he would seldom deviate. The robbers were then seen sailing towards the Chagres, where at its mouth, Negroes stated the English had anchored.

I am most grateful to John Thrower for bringing to my attention the British Library 1684 Panama City Environs Military Map. [83631(a)] Puerto del Pontón corresponds to the 700 metres wide, shallow inlet of modern-day Puerto Langosta. This can be further substantiated by the location of the islets. By being anchored off the inlet the Spaniards could have managed to drift three miles to the two keys. "Fourteen leagues" past Nombre de Dios equates with the Naranjo Keys. The Spaniards would have most likely scrambled onto the NE key: which was the closest.

Instead of pursuing boat hire at the wave-lashed village of María Chiquita, I simulated a crow's-nest view of the islets from a two-seater plane, which I had hired at Paitilla Airport in

Panama City. The vegetation comprised jungle, palms and mangroves. The plane facilitated the documentation of the neighbouring coastline, which added to a pictorial feel for a story that involved young Francis. In 1999 René Gómez provided John and me with a boat to obtain all the conceivable seaborne views. We swiftly drifted as the stiff NE Trades propelled a lather of waves. Therefore it was blatantly evident just how fast the Spaniards had drifted the five miles towards the safety of the islets, when Drake was side-tracked by the seaward vessel.

River Chagres and Casa de Las Cruces

Immediately after the "Pontón" robbery Drake, in his unswerving lust for booty, was reconnoitring the mighty Chagres. This is the main navigable artery to pierce the isthmus. Its attraction was the way station at Casa de Las Cruces. It stood on the south bank two miles NE of the river's most southern meander, being eighteen miles by trail from Panama City. Drake noted that to reach Cruces entailed nearly three days rowing from the estuary. There was a wharf and warehouses to store merchandise that was being transhipped between mules and barges, which plied between Panama City and the Atlantic coast. The Cruces trail, which still exists, linked Casa de Las Cruces to Panama City. During the dry season, mules would constantly convey the bulky merchandise on the land-leg of the journey to the way station and those Spaniards, who did not wish to walk to Nombre de Dios, would use this trail to complete their journey by water.

The Spanish sources reveal that during these years a party of English and French "pirates" raided coastal shipping and penetrated the River Chagres as far as the warehouses at Casa

de Las Cruces. Drake was the first privateer to reach the way station. The English seized clothing and other merchandise from the wharf and apparently robbed two men's property from the inn. To prevent the spread of alarm Drake sank three barges. *Drake Revived* confirms Drake's presence up the Chagres, which is its first recorded location. *"...the River of Chagro, where himselfe had beene the yeere before,..."* [Wright, 269]

The mouth of the Chagres is easily studied from the ruined post-Drake, Lorenzo fort on a forty metre high bluff. This forms the north shore of the mouth, where one is granted a splendid view. The south bank is low, sandy and backed by jungle. Today one can navigate up the beautiful, jungle-lined, serene river only for seven miles, until reaching the dam near Gatún. Here the Chagres has been flooded to widen the Panama Canal. In December 1998 René Gómez took me in his friend's speed boat from Gatún out to sea to also view the river mouth.

Rain fell all day. Therefore the excursion was repeated the following April. However we were still plagued by some rain and grey skies. There were a few minutes of bright light, that provided enough light to illuminate the jungle foliage.

In 1991 I was fortunate to visit Cruces. During my first attempt, there were no boats available for hire at Gamboa. A few days later during the second attempt, whilst hitch-hiking, I was given a lift by a group, who were to hire a fishing boat. Prior to reaching their swim, I was kindly taken the two miles in the other direction to see where the Cruces trail reaches the river. The settlement originally stood a few metres below me, because flooding from the presence of the canal has caused the level of the Chagres to be higher at this particular point.

Point San Blas

Diego Flores de Valdés, commander of the Spanish treasure fleet, writing from Nombre de Dios on 16 March, 1571, reported that, *"...an English ship with an oared pinnace is anchored off Cativa Headland, which is eighteen leagues from this port."* [Wright, 19]

This jungle covered, undulating headland, is an unmistakable landmark. Ships can find succour off the point's east and south sides. If Drake's modus operandi in 1572 and 1573 was previously implemented, Drake had spent time in 1571 hiding inside the point and amongst the San Blas archipelago.

The Central Coast

Around 3 May we read that the *"...English corsairs lay off the coast between Bastimentos, which is near Nombre de Dios, and Puerto Bello,.."*
[Interrogatory, presented at Nombre de Dios, May 15, 1571, 23]

Here lie several high, rocky, jungle-clad islets which provide numerous sheltered and secluded anchorages. Consequently the English were reported to have captured a dozen cargo ships plying between Nombre de Dios and the Chagres. This was certainly Drake, because in 1572 he left Nombre de Dios and sailed decisively to Bastimentos, as though he had intimate knowledge of where he was bound.

I studied this cluster of islets from the aforementioned aeroplane. In 1994 I passed between them in a canoe en route from Isla Grande to Portobelo.

Point San Blas

From Nombre de Dios Cristóbal de Salinas informs us that around the 8 May twenty-three Englishmen captured an advice ship from Cartagena bound for Nombre de Dios. Again there was a loss of life. The friar was stripped and the survivors were released on to one of the numerous white sand islets near the headland; from which they were subsequently rescued. The *Swan* remained in the islands, whilst Drake in the pinnace sailed for the Chagres.

River Chagres

Up the Chagres Drake encountered eighteen barks. He seized four of them carrying merchandise, which included some gold and silver. During the process, he freed Negro slaves. These would swell the ranks of those who had already escaped from the Spaniards. From their villages deep in the jungle they would launch attacks on their hated former masters. Drake was now probably thinking how he could exploit this potentially beneficial situation.

"Port Pheasant", Colombia

In late June Drake sailed into the most secluded haven on the isthmus. Here he refitted his ship for the homeward voyage and deposited stores for his anticipated return. Here he unwisely released his Spanish prisoners, who would subsequently compromise the usefulness of this haven.

Plymouth

Drake was home by October and had shown the Hawkins family that a privateering war against Spain was far more lucrative than slaving. The slaving expeditions required extensive fitting out of more ships, numerous extra men, who would engage in the dangers of capturing Negroes and the voyages lasted longer. The selling of slaves now frequently needed to be implemented by force. If trade "beyond the line" ventured into the realms of lawlessness, then privateering was just one more chilling step into the religious cold war. Drake's success had inspired other mariners. Hence he would no longer be the only Englishman in the Caribbean. However it would only be Captain Francis Drake, who would take the private war ashore to the treasure house of the world.

Chapter Five

The Caribbean Voyage of 1572-3

Plymouth

On Whitsunday Eve, the 24 May, 1572, Captain Francis Drake
in the *Pasco*, accompanied by his brother John in command of
the twenty-five ton *Swan*, weighed anchor. The total combined
crew consisted of seventy-three men, all under thirty except for
one of fifty years. The ships were lavishly victualled for one
year. Stowed below in pre-fabricated sections were three *dainty*
Pinnaces. The main destination was Nombre de Dios in
Panamá . As the ships cleared Plymouth Sound, Drake was
bound on a fairy tale voyage that was not just to make him a
living legend but an everlasting, international household name
and synonymous with every school child's education in the
Western world.

The Guadeloupe Channel

The favourable NE Trades swiftly carried the little ships across
the Atlantic and on 29 June reached Dominica and Guadeloupe
in the Caribbean, which was then still called a part of the North
Sea.

"...we entered between Dominica and Guadeloupe, where we
descried two canoas, comming from a rocky Iland three
leagues off Dominica...We landed on the south side of it,
remaining there three days to refresh our men, and water our
ships out of one of those goodly rivers, which fall downe of the
mountaine. There we saw certaine poore cottages built with

Palmito boughs and branches, but no inhabitants at that time, civill not savage, the cottages serving not for continuall inhabitation but onely for their uses that came to that place at certaine seasons to fish...The third day after, about three in the afternoone, we set saile from thence, towards the continent of Tirre firma." [D.R. 255]

There is no island within nine miles of Dominica. The nearest is about sixteen. This includes either <u>Marie Galante</u> to the NE, or the Les Saintes group to the NW. Both areas were easily reached by ferries from Guadeloupe. Of all the Drake anchorages visited so far identifying this one has proved nearly impossible.

Marie Galante cannot be described as a rocky island, since it is fertile but does have small streams on its south side, which disappear in the dry season. However Drake was here during the rainy months. Les Saintes are small rocky islands devoid of any surface water. Its inhabitants have to store rain water in cisterns. There is no sheltered anchorage on any of the south coasts. A fringing coral reef runs continuously along Marie Galante. The only slight indentation is at Port des Basses. Its entrance is almost closed by coral with a depth of 3¼ fathoms decreasing rapidly within. This would certainly have been unsuitable for Drake's three ships. There are two coves on both of the main Les Saintes Islands but they are afflicted by perennial swells. Grand Bourg, the open and main port on the SW side of Marie Galante, is the one remote possibility.

The only sheltered and incidentally the best anchorage between Guadeloupe and Dominica with a water supply, is on the NW side of Marie Galante. Sailors approaching its NE side would term it as *rocky Iland*. This enigma may be due to the less important detail slipping from memory, or to a mistranscription with regard to the south coast. On his last voyage field studies indicate that Drake used the NW coast.

Sierra Nevada, Colombia

On 6 July the environmentally unusual, soaring snow-capped peaks of Colombia's Sierra Nevada were observed in passing from ten leagues. The highest peaks are Bolívar and Colón. During the dry season, I saw traces of snow from an aircraft. The 5,775 metres peaks are about twenty-five miles inland. Consequently with the attendant cumulous clouds their sighting from the sea would be unlikely during the dry season, when much of the snow had melted. At Rodadero I hired a boat for three hours at $29 an hour. After pounding through a rough sea for an hour, we were 9.5 miles from the coast. The entire mountain range was visible but the clouds prevented the sighting of snow. However I was in Drake's wake.

Drake was here during the calm winds of the wet season, when the immense precipitation fell as snow on the peaks. However with greater cloud cover the peaks are only occasionally visible. Hence photographing snow during a limited visit would always be an uncertain and potentially a costly failure.

Drake hurried past to his secret base-camp, deep in the unexplored mountainous jungle wastes of the Darien, which now straddles the Colombian and Panamanian border. Here, the coast is steep and rocky with the occasional sandy beach. Due to two days of calms, which are typical in the rainy months, the ships did not arrive at Drake's *Port Phesant* until 12 July.

"Port Phesant", Colombia

Drake had provisioned here a year earlier on pheasants which profusely abounded. This was the first anchorage where Drake built a fort. Since this haven was unnamed, this was the first of many harbours, where Drake was to be environmentally inspired to christen an anchorage. Consequently its identification is not initially straight forward.

"...our Port Phesant, which is a fine round Bay, of verie safe harbour for all winds, lying betweene two high points, not past halfe a cables length over at the mouth, but within eight or ten cables length everie way, having ten or twelve fadome water, more or lesse, full of good fish, the soile also verie fruitfull;.." [D.R. 255-6]

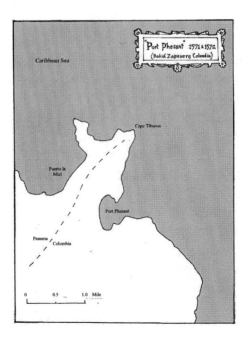

From this point onward my sleuthing was to be significantly assisted by American, Dean Edwin Webster, who lived in Panamá for twenty-four years and studied Drake's haunts as an archaeologist. He very kindly furnished me with copies of his essays. Along with Mr Aker, he identifies **Zapzurro Bay** as Drake's lair. Webster's chart studies conclude that along this stretch of coastline there are six suitable anchorages for small vessels. *"None are anywhere near 1600 yards (eight cables length) across. Only two, Zapzurro and Trigana are more than three fathoms in depth. None have entrances of only one hundred yards. Today only Zapzurro could be called a round bay lying between two high points. (It is entirely possible that in Drake's day Isla Tarena was connected to the mainland, making Bahía Gloria fit the description also, but it is only three fathoms in depth at the entrance and two fathoms within.)"* [The Webster Essays, Drake in Panamá, 1572-1573: A Geography]

I explored Bahía Gloria, which is situated thirty miles further south into Colombia. I cannot imagine that a high rocky neck of land could disappear in only 400 years and leave a navigable passage. Even if this geography existed any ship coasting northwards would have more easily discerned Drake's presence than is possible at Zapzurro. Furthermore, Webster has only flown over the Drake sites east of Narganá. Fortunately Webster continues:
" In all probability, Port Pheasant is Bahía Zapzurro, lying between two high points, seven fathoms in depth, nine hundred yards across, a little under two hundred yards between the reefs and coco palm groves at the mouth. It lies just under Cape Tiburon, easily missed by any ship standing clear of the point." [ibid]

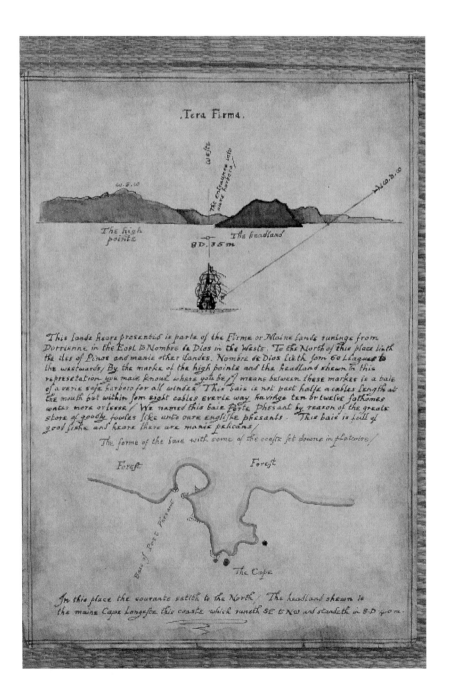

.Tera Firma.

This lande heare presentid is parte of the Firme or Maine lande runinge from Dorienne in the East to Nombre de Dios in the Weste. To the North of this place lieth the iles of Pinos and manie other ilandes. Nombre de Dios lieth som 60 Leagues to the westwards/ By the marke of the high pointe and the headland shewn in this representation you maie knowl where you be /if meane betweene these markes is a baie of a verie safe harboro for all windes. This baie is not past halfe a cables length at the mouth but within som eight cables everie way havinge ten or twelve fathomes wates more or lesse / We named this baie Porte Phesant by reason of the greate store of goodly fowles like unto oure englishe phesants. This baie is full of good fishe and heare there are manie pelicans /

The forme of the baie with some of the coaste set downe in platinor /

In this place the courante setteth to the North / The headland shewn is the maine Cape Longesse this coaste which runeth SE to NW and standeth in 8D 40m.

Nautically the haven lies four miles south of the Colombian and Panamanian border, which is formed by the 123 metre high Cape Tiburón, being of very steep rocky bluffs and capped by thick woods. The *Admiralty Pilot* also states that Bahía Zapzurro is a narrow cove and provides a good anchorage for small vessels. Care during approach is required due to patches of coral. The width of the entrance stated in *Drake Revived* probably refers to the distance between the reefs and not to the span between the points of land which is between a quarter and half a mile. Hence the width of the actual present-day navigable entrance conforms fairly closely with the contemporary account.

"There dwelt no Spanyards within thirty five leagues of that place, Tolou being neerest to the Eastwards, and Nombre de Dios to the westwards." [D.R. 255-6]

Webster writes, *"From Zapzurro it is sixty leagues to Nombre de Dios, fifty to Tolu. No other point corresponds any better to the thirty-five leagues to each given in our source."* [ibid]

Although *Port Phesant* was identified by 1972, I was the first Drake scholar to reach the haven. Despite its remote appearance on maps, one can arrive by hired canoe from Puerto Obaldía in Panamá, or in twin engine tourist launches, which ply between Zapzurro and Turbo, Colombia. Zapzurro is a village located on the NW shore, which fortunately is clear of the site where Drake built his stockade. To my surprise the economy of this hamlet and those to the south are supported by subtle, rustic, tourism. Urban Colombians come here in small groups to sample the natural quiet life.

Port Phesant was more isolated in Drake's time but, whilst rowing ashore, smoke was seen issuing from the woods. Perceiving the possible danger, Francis ordered to be accompanied by another boat. With their harquebuses primed, the English warily crept ashore, where they found a lead plate containing a message written five days earlier by a captain John Garret nailed, *"to a mightie great tree (greater then any foure men, joyning hands, could fathome about)..."* [D.R. 256] Garret had previously been here with Drake, to where they had brought the Spanish prisoners. Garret had realised that the latter had later returned and removed Drake's stores. The fire was in a neighbouring huge tree and supposedly there were still flames.

Drake's first task would have been to place sentinels on the saddle of high land leading to Cape Tiburón. Here the land is narrowest and the scouts could espy vessels approaching from west and east. Today a half mile long trail ascends the jungle mountain side to a height of 700 feet from where the aforementioned views are appreciated. From this point the *fine round Bay* is truly evident. Its shape is enhanced by the lush, mountainous tropical setting.

The day after Drake's arrival, minds were alerted by the sight of an approaching bark, owned by Sir Edward Horseyes of the Isle of Wight and commanded by James Ranse, who had sailed with Drake on the ill-fated Hawkins voyage. Some of his thirteen men crew had previously been here with Drake. Ranse was keen to join forces and accepted Drake's conditions. With increased numbers the English no doubt in one way felt more protected but realised that this anchorage was no longer safe from the enemy. Drake's overriding need was to use this perfect harbour so the carpenters could assemble the pinnaces for the

raid upon Nombre de Dios. In view of a possible attack, Drake utilised the remaining men to build a fort, *"...on a most fit plot, three-quarters of an acre of ground,.."* [D.R. 257] The monstrous trees were felled, transported by tackle and placed on top of each other until the walls were thirty feet high. The gate was at the water's edge.

"The whole plot was built in a Pentagonall forme, to wit, of five equall sides and angles, of which angles two were towards the sea, and that side betweene them was left open, for the easie launcing of our Pinnaces. The other foure equall sides were holey (excepting the gate before mentioned) firmely closed up. Without, instead of a trench, the ground was rid for fiftie foote space, round about." [ibid]

Charts show a bight tucked into the north corner of the cove. Only here is the shoreline totally concealed from ships passing close to the haven. By strategically matching the size and shape of the fort to the lie of the land, it should be possible to identify precisely, the site and orientation of the fort. For example, the base would overlook the water's edge, whilst the apex faced the gap in Cabo Tiburón. When I entered by boat, it was apparent that the theoretical site of the fort was correct. The area of ground was in concert with the narrative; the shape of which was semi-circular. Its baseline was the beach and its arc was marked where the flat ground suddenly rose. The ground was sandy and was only occupied by two rustic holiday huts. Buttress rooted trees and bushes form the bulk of the vegetation. To quench curiosity to the limit, I walked and sailed the whole perimeter of the cove looking for an alternative possibility. Drake scholars can now be assured that the site of the fort has been conclusively identified.

To gain a further appreciation, I wanted pictures overlooking the, *most fit plot,..of ground.* I scrambled up a barely discernible trail through a banana plantation. It was literally two steps up and one step back. My sweaty hands were covered in dirt, which presented a nasty threat to my brand new Nikon F4. The world's most expensive camera was now having to live up to its manufacturer's claims. By now the litre-sized canteen was empty and my thirst was intense! To add to my discomforts the trail abruptly terminated in dense undergrowth and I was not where I had intended to be. After recovering in the near motionless sea that slops on to Drake's white, sand beach, I found a more direct and slightly easier climb, where the jungle had been destroyed by fire. The absence of trees assured a clear view, when at last I was directly behind and high above the site of Drake's stockade. I was astonished how Francis Drake had found the most exacting strategic plot of ground along the whole isthmus, which was now totally encompassed in the viewfinder.

Drake was amazed how all the paths and alleys, which he cut the previous year, were now completely overgrown. The well trodden jungle trails of today provided timeless looking pictures. The English marvelled at the vegetation.

"The rest was verie thicke with trees, of which many were of those kindes which are never without greene leaves, till they are dead at the roote (excepting onely one kinde of tree amongst them, much like to our Ash, which when the sunne commeth right over them, causing great raines, suddainely casteth their leaves, viz. within three dayes, and yet within sixe dayes after becomes all greene againe)." [ibid]

On top of the mountain saddle I found such a cluster of long bare branches spouting from a trunk which resembled our English ash. I was at *Port Phesant* right at the beginning of the rainy season. Drake was here at the height of the rains. The sky was cloudy with patches of blue. After a shower the terrific wet heat returned. Perhaps it was also natural to Drake and his men, to shake these ash-like branches and refreshingly shower themselves with the evaporating droplets.

"The leaves of the other trees do also in part fal away, but so as the trees continue still greene notwithstanding, being of a marvelous height, and supported as it were with five or sixe naturall buttresses growing out of their bodies, so farre that three men may so be hidden in each of them that they which shall stand in the verie next buttresse shall not be able to see them. One of them specially was marked to have had seaven of those staies or buttresses, for the supporting of his greatnesse

and height, which being measured with a line close by the barke and neere to the ground, as it was indented or extant, was found to be above thirtie nine yards about." [ibid]

These trees still dot the landscape but are nowhere near as large. Perhaps this is due to human cultivation, which may account for the absence of pheasants. I had especially learnt this name in Spanish to facilitate their documentation. All I found were turkeys, which may have also been seen.

After a week the work was complete. Stores and armaments had been shipped aboard the pinnaces. On the morning of 20 July the entire flotilla cleared the haven and, ...*within three days arrived...* at the Isla de Pinos, which was only thirteen leagues away. Webster noted that to the reader this seemingly excessive time-frame might suggest Drake's Port Phesant is further east. However it must be remembered that Drake was sailing against the usual one knot current. Also there is normally a strong head wind, which also helps to build a choppy sea. Furthermore Drake was bringing up a fleet of diverse types of craft, which could further account for slow passage. This timing is consistent with a later sailing westwards from Isla Pinos to the Cativas. This distance of 28-30 leagues took five days. Conversely sailing east with the current and a favourable wind from Isla Bastimentos to Isla Pinos, Drake traversed these forty-eight leagues between an early morning and the evening of the next day. I was to experience such differences in my sailing times up and down the coast.

I also left *Port Phesant* by sea but sailing only seven miles as far as Puerto Obaldía in Panamá. On the village airstrip was a crippled light plane. Next day was Good Friday and no

101

fisherman wanted to go anywhere for a moderate price. As I had been informed the night before, *Transpasa Airlines* were to dispatch a plane from Panama City to repair the stranded plane's wheel. I calculated that its return flight to base would pass within sight of Pinos. My letter of introduction helped secure a free flight to Isla Soskatupo airstrip. From here I paid two Cuna Indian girls to paddle me across the bay to Sasardí village. Living on one's wits is a prerequisite when most of an expedition is not organised but relies on chance. Therefore when we were overtaken by a motorised dug-out canoe, I hailed its occupants and arranged to be taken to Pinos Island. All I had to do on reaching Sasardí was to buy drinks and change craft.

"Port Plentie" = Island of Pines, Panamá

Pinos is the largest of the San Blas Islands. This densely wooded whale-shaped island rises to a 122 metre high ridge and lies 2¼ miles NNW of Punta Sasardí. Beaches run continuously along its south and west shores and Drake was now anchored on the island's SW point, to which charts refer as Pinos Anchorage.

When Drake landed, two frigates from Nombre de Dios were being loaded with plank and timber. From the Negro workmen Drake learnt of the town's current strength. The Negroes were ferried across the two cable wide channel and put ashore on the adjacent mainland, where I found an isolated white sand beach. The mountainous nature of the landscape, ensured that no word of Drake's destination could precede his arrival.

With a sense of urgency volunteers for the raid were assembled. The remainder were charged to remain with the three ships and the caravel with captain Ranse. Drake's fifty-three men and Ranse's twenty were ferried by three well armed pinnaces and Ranse's shallop.

Cativas Island

Five days later in the morning and twenty-five leagues closer to their quarry Drake landed his men for weapon training. Drake delivered a rallying speech. He stated that Nombre de Dios was not walled, thus a weak target, and that they had the element of surprise. Around one o'clock under the blistering sun the expedition embarked upon its final outward leg.

Drake had thus nearly sailed the whole length of the San Blas archipelago. A Spanish map dated 1785, which is a composite of many earlier charts, names the islands off Point San Blas, as Cabezas or Cativas. [cited in the booklet, *The Defence of Portobelo*, Webster, E.]

A 16th century ruttier in Hakluyt, [Vol. VII. 233] states that the Cativas islands comprise, *three or four Isles*. Both groups consist of a higher number. The *South America Pilot Vol. IV* list the Cativas as including islets such as Cayos Chichime and lie 6 miles west of Cayos Holandes and on the east side of the north approach to Golfo de San Blas. This modern-day placing diametrically opposes the Webster location. Wright [xxxv] indicates that the islands took their name from the Cativas headland, to which the ruttier refers by its Spanish name as Cabeza de Cativa, which nowadays is Point San Blas.

There are many islands in this area and it is impossible to confirm upon which Drake landed. There are two strong possibilities. The SW beach on the southern Chichime Cays is a well sheltered, idyllic stretch of white sand bordered by a mirror calm sea. This beach would have been on Drake's route. The strongest contender is the kilometre long island of Porvenir. It is one mile east of Point San Blas and, like the other islands, has an anchorage on its leeward west side. Approaching Porvenir from the east constitutes a majestic picture as Point San Blas boldly presents itself in the immediate background.

"Rio Francisco"

Before sunset, Drake had swiftly reached the *River Francisco*, being about twenty-six miles from Chichime Cays or twenty-one from Porvenir. The factors of time and distance are vital in trying to locate Cativas Island. In the given time frame it would seem that Drake must have sailed from Porvenir in order to reach the *Rio Francisco* before dark. This information is also crucial in trying to establish the identification of this major river. The latter appears on all the colonial maps but in various places and unfortunately its name has changed. At this stage of the book I purport that this river is the **Cuango**, which, by hard rowing under sail could have been reached half an hour before sunset, which was 6.30 pm.

Viento Frio

In 1991 to retrace Drake's approach to Nombre de Dios from the Cativas, I was lucky enough to hire the same canoe which I had used during my three days of exploration around the western San Blas Islands. Like Drake we sailed hard by the shore, which was backed by jungle-forested hills. By being near the coast Drake's presence could not be discerned by any harbour lookouts at the entrance to Nombre de Dios bay. When I was abreast of the village of Viento Frio, within five miles of Nombre de Dios, I was sensitive to the fact that, here Drake anchored to await being enveloped by the deepest shade of night.

"...being come within two leagues of the point of the Bay, he caused us to strike a hull and cast our grappers, riding so untill the darke night." [D.R. 260]

For photographic purposes I had to be here during daylight. The following year in the same canoe I retook the picture to simulate darkness by using a dark blue filter coupled with a one stop underexposure.

Nombre de Dios

"Then we waighed againe and set saile, rowing hard aboard the shore, with as much silence as we could, till we recovered the point of the harbour under the high land: there we stayed all silent, purposing to attempt the towne in the dawning of the day, after we had reposed our selves for a while." [ibid]

To enter the half mile wide Nombre de Dios Bay small vessels can use the channel between Point Pescador and the palm covered Cayo Cuili. El Peñon, a hill of forty-four metres, is the *high land*. Reefs ensure that the bay is entered by larger vessels one mile north of Punta Pescador.

Nombre de Dios was named by Diego de Niqueza around 1510. When Niqueza stepped ashore, his utterance of, "Here we will found a settlement in the name of God." gave rise to its name.

[Masefield, *On The Spanish Main*, 1906, 10] Nombre de Dios soon became crucial for Spanish commerce and conquest. The South Sea, today known as the Pacific Ocean, was discovered in 1513. By 1519 a shorter route was desired to link the two oceans. An old trans-isthmus Indian trail had been found at Nombre de Dios, which led towards the new city of Panamá on the Pacific coast. Nombre de Dios was settled in 1520 and work began to widen the trail. When in the 1530s silver and gold was discovered in present-day Bolivia and Perú, Nombre de Dios became a treasure terminus. The treasure arrived by mule train and was briefly stored before being shipped to Seville. From Spain supplies to make the colonial life more comfortable were unloaded. Due to exposure to the prevailing northerly winds and its shallow bay, the settlement remained small. To further put Drake's assault into context it is useful to refer to Baptista Antonio's description, which he wrote in 1584, but could have been virtually written today.

"Nombre de Dios is builded upon a sandy Bay hard by the sea side, it is a citie of some thirtie householdes or inhabitants: their houses are builded of timber...it is full of woods and some places of the land are overflown with water continually by reason of much raine which doth fall upon the hils."
[Hakluyt, Vol. VII, 115]

The heavy rains and the shelter afforded by the hills from the refreshing trade winds provided a breeding ground for disease. This is exacerbated at night, when the land breeze cancels out the sea breeze.

In 1981 I had to reach the present-day village by fording the River Nombre de Dios on foot and walking a mile along a jungle trail. My stride was interrupted by a long thin snake with blue stripes down its sides, as it slithered just in front of my path. This was no doubt a regular sight for Drake. Two years later the village was reached by a gravel road but the river Nombre de Dios still had to be forded. Nowadays, a bridge provides a welcome finishing touch to easing the traveller's passage. My definitive visit was embellished by aerial photography.

Drake's plan was to attack at dawn. The men were dwelling upon the exaggerated reports of the town's strength and size, which had been rumoured by the Negroes on Pinos Island. Therefore Drake in his spontaneous wisdom decided to soothe his men's nerves and attacked upon arrival under moon light at 3am. Inside the bay a newly arrived supply ship spotted Drake's four pinnaces as they were hastily rowed towards the yellow sand beach. The ship's gundalow was driven to the east shore to abort the spreading of the alarm. The English landed unopposed since the posted gunner fled to alert the town. As Drake leapt ashore, he also stepped into the history books. He was to become the most dashing, daring man of his age and thus an inspirational figure to his contemporaries. The cries of the inhabitants were amplified by the ringing of the church bell and the roll of drums. Twelve men were left at the pinnaces to guard the retreat.

"And having made sure work of the Platform before he would enter the Towne, hee thought best first to view the Mount on the East side of the Towne, where he was informed by sundry intelligences the yeere before they had an intent to plant Ordnance, which might scowre round about the Towne. Therefore, leaving one halfe of his company to make a stand at the foot of the Mount, he marched up presently unto the top of it, with all speed, to try the truth of the report for the more safetie. There wee found no peece of Ordnance, but onely a verie fit place prepared for such use, and therefore we left it without any of our men, and with all celeritie returned downe the Mount." [D.R. 261]

Despite having been to Nombre de Dios three times during ten years, the location of this mount still puzzled me. The only hill is the already mentioned El Peñon, which is a mile to the NNE and too far to reach once the inhabitants were preparing to defend themselves, when the object of the attack was to use the element of surprise. I concluded that this mount could have been a man-made earthworks. However after my 1990 visit correspondence from Dean Edwin Webster dispelled the puzzle.

In 1976 the Panamanian government sponsored the resettlement of some nearby landless farmers. From clearing the undergrowth 500 metres to the west of the present-day village the site of the colonial city was unearthed! This meant that the two hills to the west of the present-day settlement featured significantly during Drake's two raids. Webster has found three contemporary maps. A mound called the Morro, is shown protruding into the sea behind which, is a hill where the proposed fort was later built. As I stood on this sculptured 34 metre high, flat hilltop, it was a spiritual realisation to know that Francis Drake stood here moments before his legendary career began.

Excavation also proved that the sea has receded. The remains of two Spanish ships were found; one of which was buried eight metres under the sand about 75 metres inland from the present shore. Similarly, the Morro is now over 100 metres from the beach. The town stretched from the Morro and the hill to the estuary of the River Nombre de Dios. Its configuration measured about 200 x 300 metres. The town's western edge was disturbed in 1959 with the building of an airstrip. In the late 1980s a road was taken into the modern village over the disused airstrip. Much of the Morro was bulldozed to provide soil for the jetty, from which the manganese was shipped.

"Then our Captaine appointed his brother, with John Oxnam and sixteene other of his men, to goe about behinde the Kings treasure-house, and enter neere the Easter end of the market-place; himselfe with the rest, would passe up the broad street, into the market-place, with sound of Drum and Trumpet."
[ibid]

During the excavations, the stones of the principal street re-emerged. The positions of the houses were established by pottery shards and pieces of metal. All discovered artefacts were eventually lodged in the National Museum. However the site was not thoroughly excavated. Also Dean Webster retired and returned to the USA. Until then, the site had not been disturbed, due to the simple method of agriculture; that of machete, fire and planting stick. Today, the site to the east of the road is a 100 metre square of empty bare earth and sand. To the west, between the road and the river, is a coconut plantation. This area has never been excavated. A renewed dig would more than likely enable the actual plan of the town to be pieced together. This would herald a major colonial, archaeological, achievement, which would enable Drake's foot steps to be very accurately followed.

In April 1993, a small manganese mine was operating on the empty square. Amid the disturbed soil were pottery shards, the neck of an olive jar and ships' nails. I was taken into the coconut plantation, where I stood in a metre deep hole next to the walled foundation. I wrenched out large pieces of green, glazed pots, that were probably here during Drake's last voyage, since very soon afterwards, the settlement was abandoned. John Thrower sent photographs of his finds to The British Museum, which confirmed the artefacts dated from the late 16th century. By 1998 the mining had ceased. Some rusty equipment ensured that the square was somewhat spoilt.

The present-day village is also laid-out around its main square, which is within fifty metres of the beach. The streets cross the square at right angles, running west to east and north to south. By standing next to the white-washed church, looking across the sandy square towards the sea, it is still possible to almost "feel" and "see" the skirmish unfolding in one's mind.

Drake's two divisions gave the Spaniards the impression of being attacked by a larger force. Due to the delay in examining the mount, the Spaniards had time to assemble on the SE side of the market square, near the governor's house and the town gate, from which led the road to Panamá. Drake's force was driven back by a volley of shot. Drake's brother arrived with his division from the east of the square.

This pincer attack forced most of the colonists to flee the town through the aforementioned gate.

Amazingly, and indeed right on the SE corner of the original town, remains the beginning of the Camino Real, which translates as Royal Road. It is nothing more than a tree lined trail but Drake very well knew that over its baked red mud plodded the mule trains burdened with Spain's fabulous riches.

The church bell continued to ring and Drake would not damage the barricaded church to evict the remaining defendants. Several prisoners were forced to show Drake where the silver was stored. Beyond the great door of the governor's house, where the mules were unladen, candlelight revealed piles of silver bars, each estimated to weigh between thirty-five and forty pounds and occupying an area of seventy feet by ten and by twelve feet in height. Drake ordered his men not to remove any bars whilst some defendants still remained in the town.

Furthermore it was also desired to enter the more impregnable King's treasure house, which was nearer the beach, since the more valuable commodity of gold, pearls and jewels meant less weight for value would need to be carried.

It is difficult to believe that Drake saw anywhere near the amount of silver stated. It was more than likely that the beach-side treasure house was empty because the treasure was only brought to Nombre de Dios from Panamá once the flotilla from Spain had arrived. In 1572 it had arrived on 5 January. This was the beginning of the dry season when the muddy trail began to dry-out, which made the passage of the mule trains much easier. Furthermore, the Spaniards would not have left treasure in vast quantities in such a vulnerable place as Nombre de Dios, which was often threatened by corsairs. It is possible that the amount was exaggerated to stimulate the reader of "this Dull or Effeminate Age to follow his Noble steps for Gold and Silver" as the title piece of *Drake Revived* includes. Nonetheless, some silver must have been evident for Drake to have launched the raid.

As *Drake Revived* was edited and most likely sharpened by Drake, it is conceivable that the raid has been somewhat dramatised. By editing Drake tended to agree that Nombre de Dios was the size of Plymouth. A comparison of 16th century maps proves that even in Drake's day, he had raided a small settlement. This term is supported by the fact, that Nombre de Dios had a transient population. Its numbers swelled from around thirty when the annual treasure fleet was due. Notwithstanding it has been the implications of the raid, coupled with Drake's audacity and not the military aspects that captured the imagination of his contemporaries and biographers.

As the English re-grouped a resident Negro called Diego informed Drake that their pinnaces could be captured due to the number of Spaniards remaining. The pinnace guards were nervous when the higher than expected numbers of defendants tried to re-group. A storm interrupted the renewed exchange of fire as powder and bow strings were temporarily rendered useless. Drake told his jittery band that he had brought them, "to the mouth of the treasure of the world," and that they must blame themselves if they failed. These words rang a sense of irony. As soon as the torrential rain ceased, Drake ordered the treasure house to be taken by his brother and John Oxenham's division, whilst he held the square. To everyone's surprise Drake fainted. He had been shot in the thigh by a arquebus ball during the initial skirmish and to keep his men's spirits high, had told nobody. Blood was now seen to trickle into the sand. The life of their much needed captain was worth more than the pursuit of booty and they eventually persuaded Drake to board the pinnaces. The raiders joined by Diego, carried the many wounded, leaving behind the dead trumpeter. Enough fit men were able to capture and bring along the Spanish ship which had anchored earlier. The first priority was to restore the strength of the wounded. Drake directed his men to Bastimentos Island, where he knew from his voyages of reconnaissance, that the beach would serve as a defendable refuge.

"Isla Bastimentos" = Isla Grande

"Ile Bastimientes, or The Ile of Victuales, which is an Iland that lieth without the Bay to the Westwards, about a league off the Towne, where we stayed the next dayes, to cure our wounded men, and to refresh ourselves in the goodly Gardens which we there found, abounding with great store of all daintie rootes and fruites, besides great plentie of Poulterie and other Fowles,..." [D.R. 267]

In 1983 I felt convinced that I had found Bastimentos Island. It was the wet season and, like Drake's experience, the stillness of the night was ruptured by the clattering of torrential rain battering the roof tops. A little after daybreak in clearing skies my hired boatman took me NW to the two rocky, rounded, tree-clad islets, which were clearly visible from Nombre de Dios. They were the Mogote de Afuera and Mogote de Adentro, which mean outer and inner knolls respectively. They lie between half and a mile ENE of Point Manzanillo. The outer eleven metre high islet had no beach. On the landward side of the inner, forty-one metre high islet was a shady beach. The pounding swell made the landing a tricky affair, so a very carefully timed approach was crucial. Whilst I explored ashore, the boatman safely waited out in the channel.

The beach was only fifty metres long. The island was steep, blessed with fresh water and coconuts but was too small to support gardens. However, because these islets were located at twice the stated league and were the closest to Nombre de Dios, I discounted the possibility of exploring islands further west. Over the ensuing years I had positively found anchorages, which in some cases, were at odds with the stated distances. Therefore I pondered over the plausibility of my identification. Locating Bastimentos was the first time that I had worked from a contemporary estimated distance and I felt bound to accept initially, that Bastimentos Island was Mogote de Adentro. Furthermore, archival research somewhat supported my findings. On one colonial map in the Canal Zone library this islet was marked as Bastimentos. However, as is typical of ancient charts, Bastimentos was not always shown to be in the same place and in most cases it was positioned towards Isla Grande - two miles further on!

Before my return in 1991 more doubt struck my mind, when I read a 16th century ruttier in Hakluyt, [Vol. VII. 223] *"...And to the West of the harbor* [Nombre de Dios] *thou shalt see two or three Islands called Islas de los Bastimentos."*

Bastimentos is a Spanish word for a supply of provisions. The one mile long **Isla Grande** happens to lie off Port Bastimentos. The island was used as a market garden for the inhabitants of Nombre de Dios and, from my observations by land and air, is the only island to support such a commodity. The island is very fertile as described and like other havens must have inspired these following words, *"Many strange Birds, Beasts and Fishes, besides Fruits, Trees, Plants, and the like, were seene."* [D.R. 326] I was lucky to photograph a parrot, which Drake must have seen in Panamá, and possibly whilst on this island.

A heavy swell rolls along the shallow, 400 metre wide channel between the mainland and the island, which is crossed by little ferry boats, leaving from the mainland hamlet of La Guayra. By sea, Drake would have cleared the reefs issuing from the north shore of Cayo Tambor, meaning Drum Key, as the channel in between the two islands was also fouled by coral beneath a confused sea of tide rips. The only anchorage suitable for small vessels is the SW side of the island, which is bound by a 400 metre long semi-circular, white, fine sand beach, gently kissed by transparent turquoise wavelets. Drake could have hidden his ships from any passing Spaniards by anchoring them behind the SW point of the island in the entrance to the mainland channel, as he had done on Pinos.

On the NE end of Isla Grande, at 305 feet, is a lighthouse. From here the visitor can study Drake's rounding of Cayo Tambor. To further ensure his safety whilst convalescing, Drake would have posted sentinels on the rocky NE shore of the island, which also commands an excellent view of the Mogotes. Here one can appreciate how the lookouts would

have sighted a pursuing Spaniard, when he had come within
two miles.

Drake Revived relates how a Spanish envoy was sent by the
governor of Nombre de Dios to ascertain by whom they had
been attacked. The English were suspected, as according to the
emissary, the French had been discounted because they would
have killed more Spaniards than was necessary and used
different arrows. The Spaniard was relieved to realise that the
English had not poisoned their arrows. The envoy commented
upon such an audacious raid being executed by so few men.
They knew of an English captain, who over the previous two
years had gained a reputation for humanely treating his
prisoners. The Spaniard wished to know if it were the same
Captain Drake. It is interesting to note that in none of the
published Spanish accounts is the envoy's spying mission
included, nor is Drake mentioned by name. Instead the Spanish

dispatches only refer to the invaders by their nationalities. This point has never been raised by biographers. One may justifiably conclude that Drake was dramatising the rise of his fame to impress the queen, to whom he was to present *Drake Revived*. It is quite plausible that this story was fabricated.

The text continues to relate how the emissary wished to arrange for Drake to receive victuals. Drake replied that the island's provisions would suffice and that the only offerings which interested him were treasure, without which he would not return home. Until Drake's wound was apparent, the envoy wondered why Drake had left behind more than 360 tons of silver and the precious gold. The Spaniard was dined and, as he departed, felt highly honoured carrying Drake's gifts.

The envoy had declared that Nombre de Dios was more interested in building its defences than pursuing Drake. However, because this anchorage was right on the busy Spanish shipping route between Nombre de Dios and the River Chagres, young Francis was thus eager to convalesce on his distant and secluded hideaway. Hence he departed next day for Pinos Island. He sent his brother along with Ellis Hixom westward to scour the Chagres for provisions and intelligence relating to the movement of valuable cargo.

By air and sea I had documented for certain the entire Bastimentos group and that Isla Grande, although being seven miles from Nombre de Dios, was the island upon which Drake convalesced. This has been confirmed by Webster's *Drake in Panamá: A Geography.* [op. cit.]

Isla de Pinos

Drake's party arrived back at base on 1 August. The next week was spent recovering from wounds and reorganising. By the eighth day the pinnaces returned from the Chagres and in vague terms *Drake Revived* states that they had fulfilled their mission. The desired intelligence, which as it transpired, was not utilised.

Captain Rance dissolved their partnership because the raid had alerted the Spaniards. The element of surprise was lost and they were now hunted men. Whilst Rance presumably returned home, Drake by contrast was preparing his ships for another offensive.

Drake and his men were now living in thatched huts on the island's SW corner. Today this site is still occupied by a primitively constructed hamlet.

I spent the night in the island's only village, which is a kilometre to the NW. I was summoned to the conference hut to explain my presence and Francis Drake's association with the island. The village school teacher knew of Francis Drake. However it was a revelation to the chief and the 200 assembled Cuna that for two months Drake had used the island as his base. It was a wonderful experience standing before an entire tribe - like something out of an adventure film. The entire experience unfolded in my mind, when two Easters later I flew low, gazing at the island's south shore.

Cartagena, Colombia

Drake had now organised two ships and three pinnaces bound for Cartagena. They left on 7 August. Seasonal calms meant that the 180 mile voyage took six days. During the evening of the 13th they anchored, *"betweene the Ilands of Charesha and Saint Barnards. Our Captaine led the three Pinnaces about the Iland, into the Harbour of Carthagene where, at the very entry, hee found a Frigate at anchor..."* [D.R. 270]

The frigate would have been anchored just inside Hicacos Point. To retain his discreet presence, Drake entered the lagoon through Boca Chica, which according to Batista Antonio, was then fifteen fathoms deep. [Hakluyt, Vol. VII. 111] Its depth would have easily accommodated the shallow draft of a pinnace, which was to reconnoitre shallow inland waters. Drake then sailed along the east side of Cares Island, also known as Tierra Bomba Island, until reaching the inner harbour, which is just north of Boca Grande. Largely due to Drake's raids Boca Chica and Cartagena were later heavily fortified. Two well preserved forts dominate Boca Chica. During the crossfire, the higher battlements on the north shore enabled the canons to destroy the masts of enemy shipping, whilst the guns on the low ramparts of the south bank, pierced the hulls.

Day tours to the Rosario Islands pass through Boca Chica, where the land is low, undulating and densely clad with trees and bushes. There are also daily boat trips to Boca Chica. The four hour stay permits careful study. Both excursions allowed the following drama to be documented.

There was only an old mariner aboard the frigate, who notified Drake that a few hours earlier, a pinnace had hastily entered the harbour enquiring if any English or French interlopers had appeared. Also that *"within the next point,"* [D.R. 271] there was a large ship from Seville. This was the inner harbour, which is now called Bahía de las Animas. The Spaniard was made to identify the vessel. The crew were locked below and the vessel cheekily towed from right under the Spanish guns to, *"...without the Iland, into the sound right afore the Towne,.."* [ibid] Horsemen cut off Drake's exit from Cartagena Bay. They *"came downe to the very point of the wood and discharged their Calviers,.."* [ibid] Martín de Mendoza confirms that this was at *"Point Hicacos, which is at the mouth of this city's harbour, where the said frigate had grounded".* [43] On this occasion Drake left empty-handed.

The flat point is about fifty metres wide. It is occupied by a light beacon and a well preserved post-Drake blockhouse.

The next day, which was the 14th, south of Cartagena two frigates were captured, aboard which was a despatch. It intended to warn Cartagena that an Englishman would have captured Nombre de Dios, if he had not been wounded in the leg and that the city should brace itself. Drake set the Spaniards ashore and proceeded southwards.

San Bernados Islands

"...so bare thence with the Ilands of Saint Bernards, about three leagues off the towne, where we found great store of fish for our refreshing." [D.R. 272]

The towne must refer to <u>Tolú</u> and not to Cartagena, which is more like twenty-five leagues away. The tiny isolated palm-mangrove islands are conveniently reached by daily boat trips from Tolú, that stop at one of the very few beaches within the islands. The white sand is kissed by transparent blue sea. To the modern-day visitor Drake had spent just over a day in paradise but this concept of environmental bliss was seldom portrayed in any of the Drake narratives and was never graphically described.

Despite being discovered, Drake was determined to remain in the Spanish Main until returning home rich. To facilitate swift movement in adequately manned vessels, he streamlined his fleet. That night Drake secretly instructed Thomas Moone the carpenter of the *Swan* to bore holes near her keel. The next morning, Drake invited his brother; the ship's captain, to accompany him fishing. John gladly accepted. From their fishing boat, Francis casually remarked how low in the water his brother's bark was floating. The pumps were manned in vain until three in the afternoon. Because the crew were very attached to their ship, Drake correctly realised that reasons for his re-organising would be better received once the ship was sunk.

Darien Sound

Drake wanted the Spaniards to think that he had cleared their coasts. Therefore the next morning being the 16 August, Drake sailed for what is today known as the Gulf of Uraba. They arrived on the 21st with the aim of hiding their ship, whilst they scoured the main in pinnaces. Beforehand fifteen days were spent careening and fitting out pinnaces and clearing the ground of trees for the building of huts. Diego's knowledge of construction was much valued. The smiths were busy at their forges repairing and manufacturing weapons. The men retained their fighting edge with archery practice and relaxed by playing quoits and bowls. The company was divided in two and rotated daily, so that days alternated between work and leisure. The food comprised, *fish, birds, hogs, deer* and the ever-present *connie*.

*All we are told regarding this location, is that Drake "had chosen a fit and convenient road (out of all trade) for our purpose,.." * [D.R. 274]

Charts show that Cape Tiburón would mark the southern limit of the main shipping route between 16th century Panamá and Colombia. From his chart Mr. Aker favours Triganá cove as best fitting a fit and convenient road. To cover every possibility all the suitable anchorages had to be recorded. Since the coast is either flat and open or mountainous with shallow indented bays, Mr Aker correctly calculated only three possible anchorages.

The gulf's entrance is twenty-eight miles wide. The distance off the main shipping lines could be up to thirty-two miles. This is one of the most vaguely described Drake anchorage and is impossible to identify positively. According to the *South American Pilot Vol. IV* the shore is, *"...low, heavily wooded and swampy on the E, S and SW sides; the N part of the W shore is steep and rocky, with coves and sandy beaches."* For Drake's purpose the NW side would be the most attractive.

Twelve miles south of Cape Tiburón is a near two mile long bay at <u>Acandí</u>. This is the largest village in the region. There is a rocky islet which nearly joins the bay's northern point, thus forming a tranquil haven. Between the point and the river is a 350 yard long sand-gravel beach backed by flat land, which would have been ideal for an encampment. The ships would not have been seen by vessels heading south. The jungle backdrop of the hook-shaped headland may have camouflaged Drake's ships from coasters on a northerly course.

Thirteen miles further in, at twenty-five miles from Cape Tiburón is the totally sheltered mile long by a ½ mile deep Triganá cove. I found no fresh water. However, there is flat ground at the cove's northern end, adjacent to which ships could be safely and discreetly anchored.

Alternatively seven miles further on, being thirty-two miles from the shipping routes, is a quarter mile wide cove, with three fathoms of water. The anchorage is protected by the 208 feet high Tarena Island a quarter of a mile to seaward. The island would partially conceal Drake's ships. A stream borders the south side of a small area of flat ground, which was occupied by a homestead.

When the tourist speed boats reached Titumate, 2½ miles to the north, they crossed the gulf for Turbo. Consequently in Titumate I hired a canoe to reach Tarena Island. Drake could not have anchored any further south because the coast is open, low and comprises mangrove swamps and shoals. As I sailed back into distant Panamá, I felt sure that I had documented Drake's mysterious haven. I had closely studied every metre of coastline, which apart from the occasional scars of slash and burn and the rustic hamlets, is unaltered since Drake's passing.

"Two leagues west of Rio Grande"

On 5 September, Drake left the ship under the charge of his
brother John and in two pinnaces headed for the store houses
along the Rio Grande de la Magdalena. To conceal his
lingering presence, Drake sailed out of sight of Cartagena.
Three days later, *"...when wee were within two leagues of the*
River, wee landed to the Westwards on the maine, where we
saw great store of Cattle." The Indians who spoke broken
Spanish, obliged Drake's needs and easily rounded up the
cattle, *"...as if they had a speciall commandment over them,*
whereas they would not abide us to come neere them."
[D.R. 275]

Armed with GPS I returned to Flores, a suburb of Barranquilla,
in 1998, to hire a boat because the previous land-based study
had not pinpointed the anchorage. For 5.8 miles west of the
river the coast is flat, rather exposed and the water is shallow,
which causes the waves to tumble vigorously. Upon returning
to Flores I realised that I had been deceived in measuring *Two*
leagues west of Rio Grande. This was because land reclamation
and boulders placed to prevent erosion had pushed the river
mouth five miles seaward. Longshore drift has resulted in river
sediment being deposited parallel to the shore for these 5.8
miles. Consequently the offshore beach is backed by lagoons
and marshes. If Drake anchored within *Two leagues* of the river
mouth, the drastic change in shoreline composition has
completely altered what he saw. Our boat could not approach
the entrance to the most easterly lagoon. I hired a small boat
from within the lagoon. Despite its shallow draft, it could not
reach the sea. Drake may have entered the lagoon during its
formation or enjoyed open access to the mainland beach before

the onset of longshore drift. I walked 2.8 miles along the offshore beach to the end of the swamps at Salgar. For the next .7 mile the land rises. At 6.5 miles west of the original river mouth, that was approximately at Flores, a rocky headland shelters the village of <u>Salgar</u> .5 mile further west. Despite not being within *Two leagues* of the river mouth, but near enough, this is the most likely place where Drake came ashore. Even here, the shallows caused the waves to thunder towards the sandy beach. However I have not seen the sea in the calms of the wet season.

The inland near Salgar is a sandy plain supporting bushes and cactus. Cattle still roam in abundance. My experiences were like Drake's. In my attempts to photograph the cattle they ran off! I gave chase through the bush. Eventually, the four cows stopped, turned around and looked into the camera, as if asking what right I had to bother them. I wiped the sweat from my brow realising that I had added a more unusual dimension to the collection of pictures.

"Rio Grande"de la Magdalena

"That same day we departed thence to Rio Grand, where wee entred about three of the clocke in the after-noone. There are two entrings into this River, of which wee entred the Westermost called Boca Chica. The freshet of this River is so great that we, being halfe a league from the mouth of it, filled fresh water for our beverage." [D.R. 276]

From the hired boat from Flores I noted that the river mouth is flanked by navigation lights, on top of high masts. Otherwise, due to the flat shore and the artificial shoreline of boulders, the mouth is hard to discern; especially in a rough sea. The original *two enterings* could have been due to the river depositing sediment, that formed a longitudinal bar. Today there is only one entrance. The mainland behind the east bank protrudes further seaward than the west bank. Hence behind the boulders of the west bank is the lagoon. However slightly up-river from Barranquilla, an impression of two channels is given by vast green floating islands of vegetation and by neighbouring swamps. This may have resembled the original mouth.

A track runs alongside the west bank towards the mouth, along which for my safety, I travelled by taxi. Muggings abound, as I had personally experienced during my visit in 1981. At nightfall two thieves tried to snatch my wrist chronometer in nearby Barranquilla. Recently, at this river mouth a ship had ran aground. It was ransacked before the authorities arrived. Therefore I took the pictures with some haste. As boat hire was then considered unnecessary, I chartered a taxi all morning for £6. It was good value, because I was also taken to, "two leagues west." The river water is always brown and is salt free around two miles up-river but not inviting or safe to drink today.

"From three a clocke till darke night we rowed up the streame, but the current was so strong downewards that wee got but two leagues all that time." [Ibid]

This corresponds to the position of the sprawling city of Barranquilla. However the other side of the river is rustic and lush.

By watching the speed of the flotsam, which is usually small trees and clusters of branches, that have been wrenched from their habitat by the mighty river, one can sympathise with the toils of Drake's party as they sweated in the steamy, stifling heat of Colombia's rainy season. I had previously been here in the wet season and was now enjoying the sunny dry season. Although the temperature only drops from 33^0 to 30^0 centigrade, the humidity is far lower and bearable.

"Wee moared our Pinnaces to a tree that night, for that presently, with the closing of the evening, there fell a monstrous shower of raine, with such strange claps of thunder and flashes of lightning,.." [ibid]

The sailors were marvelled by such an event. Drake rightly told them that from his previous experiences such storms lasted three-quarters of an hour. In the following calm the party was afflicted by mosquitoes. Their bites were relieved by lemon juice, which I also used.

Such was the motivation to become rich through plunder, the perpetual discomforts were readily tolerated by our bold ancestors. Ironically I was paying to follow Drake and had to endure hardships on a shoestring. I was constantly sweating under the load of an eighteen kilogram rucksack, as the infernal ball mercilessly beat down upon me, whilst walking and hitch-hiking through the upwelling of sultry air currents. I realised that Drake could at least hug the sea breeze. My hardships were tolerated in my unswerving quest to document one man's entire life.

"At the breake of day on the Sept. 9. we departed, rowing in the eddy, and haling up by the trees where the eddy failed, with great labour,.." [ibid]

Isolated trees of about three metres in height grow right on the river bank. The swirls of water are conspicuous. The NE wind blows against the flow of the river and the subsequent troubled water added to Drake's difficulty.

At three in the afternoon the expedition found itself five leagues up-river.

"...on the side of the River, whose channell is twentie five fathome deepe, and his bredth so great that a man can scanty be discerned from side to side." [ibid]

Drake was in the middle of the river and was signalled to go ashore by a Spaniard who was standing by some houses. Upon noticing fairer complexions he fled, inadvertently leaving Drake to help himself to a wide range of foods in the store houses.

At Sabanagrande I hired a motor launch and was sped down-river. Once I was 15 miles south of the original site of the river mouth, I began taking timeless pictures of the serene water and the flat countryside over a distance of five miles. I debarked at Soledad, where urbanisation encroaches upon the west bank. I found a wooden dilapidated store house on the river bank with a row boat moored nearby. This and views of the river bank from the road bridge, helped to thoroughly pictorially preserve Drake's penetration of Colombia's major river.

Drake was eventually driven away from the store houses. That night he anchored a league down river. Next day on the 10th, *"...wee rowed downe to the mouth of the River, where wee unladed all our provisions and cleansed our Pinnaces...and the same day went to the Westward."* [D.R. 277]

The river mouth is so remote that Drake with his boats unloaded had nothing to fear from the thinly populated Spaniards. Moreover Drake would have discerned them from a long way off.

The present-day river mouth possesses sand beaches backed by swamps and fields. I could have been in the exact position, since the west bank may have been more susceptible to erosion, due to the current driving the river water westwards.

En route back to Panamá, Drake rifled more shipping. Meanwhile John Drake seems to have left the Gulf of Darien and returned to *Port Plentie*, so-named because of the accumulating stocks of provisions.

"Port Plentie", Pinos Island, Panamá

On 14 September Captain Francis returned to *Port Plentie*, to restock his main victualling magazines with the spoils from the ships, which he had boarded between Nombre de Dios and Cartagena. He landed the wine, *cassava*, dried *beef* and *fish*, live *sheep*, *hogs* and *hens*. There was so much remaining and, to ensure their survival in case *Port Plentie* was discovered, four other store houses were built on the mainland and on the San Blas Islands, over a distance of eighty miles. There was sufficient provisions not just to supply the needs of Drake but those of his future allies, the French and the *cimarrones*.

Once Diego had joined Drake he was keen that his fellow-men should bolster Drake's cause. As arranged, in Drake's absence, John Drake accompanied Diego to organise a rendezvous with the *cimarrones*. These were the runaway Black slaves, who had taken refuge deep in the rain forest, from where they launched reprisal hit-and-run attacks against their former Spanish masters. Their numbers grew by freeing those in slavery. Their hatred for the Spaniards, knowledge of the terrain and logistical support, were to provide the platform for the phenomenal materialistic success of the voyage. This was to launch Drake towards future legendary achievements.

"River Diego"

When Francis returned to Pinos, his brother presented him with two *cimarrones*, whom he had received in exchange for two Englishmen, who acted as guarantors for the *cimarrones*. As a result of hearing about Drake's previous voyages, they were as keen to form an alliance. From Pinos on the evening of 13 September in a pinnace, Captain Francis sailed with his brother, who had arranged the rendezvous at a river named *Diego*, situated midway between Pinos and the Cabezas.

Webster identifies this river as the present-day Diablo, which is adjacent to the islands of Narganá and Corazón de Jesús. His identification is based upon the previously cited 1785 map. Webster writes, *"Just off San Blas Point are two groups of islands separated, on modern charts, by the Holandes Channel...Our account reads rather consistently if,..we take the Cabezas to be the first and the Cativas the second group. For example, the stated distance from the Isles of Pines to the* Iland *of Cativaas is given as twenty-five leagues. (see Wright, 259) It*

131

is twenty-eight leagues to the nearest group, thirty-one to Holandes Channel. The Cabezas would be the logical name for those neare the headland, since Cabeza means head in Spanish." [The Webster Essays, Drake in Panamá, 1572-1573: A Geography]

Drake had ordered his ship and pinnaces to follow next day, as his brother had found an excellent anchorage, which is characteristic of this stretch of coastline.

"...a most goodly and plentifull Countrey, and yet inhabited not with one Spaniard, or any for the Spaniards, but especially in that it lieth among a great many goodly Ilands full of Trees, where, though there be channels, yet there are such Rockes and shoales that no man can enter by night, without great danger, nor by day without discovery, whereas our Ship might lie hidden within the Trees." [D.R. 280]

Although the Spaniards knew these islands were home to interlopers, they were safe amid the myriad of shallows and reefs, which made their pursuit very dangerous.

Drake arrived the next day, the 14th. This distance could have been covered by 9am as with the wind, Drake could have easily been sailing at four knots. Drake was welcomed by a delegation at the estuary and taken one mile up-river to be entertained. Two more men were exchanged with the intent of rounding up another band at the unidentifiable River *Guana*.

Aker places the former river somewhere further east. The only crumb of comfort I gained by studying this mystery is that all the rivers look the same.

"Port Plentie", Pinos Island

Later that day Francis sailed eastwards to find his trailing ship, which he did on the 16th. Deterred by a storm she had returned to Pinos, where repairs and trimming were carried out. On the 18th, *"...our Captaine sent away one of his Pinnaces towards the bottome of the Bay, amongst the shoales and sandy Ilands, to sound out the channell for the bringing in of our Ship neere the maine."* [ibid]

There is no bay as such adjacent to Pinos. However from what follows, they were dispatched to the bottom of the Gulf of San Blas.

"Fort Diego"

"The next day we followed, and were with warie pilatage directed safely into the best channel, with much adoe to recover the Roade, among so many flats and shoales. It was neere about five leagues from the Cativaas, betwixt an Iland and the maine, where we moared our ship. The Iland was not above foure Cables length from the maine, being in quantitie some three Acres of ground, flat and very full of trees and bushes." [ibid, 280]

It appears that Drake was near the *Diego* river. Following the theories of his present position, the *Rio Diego* could have been even further west. According to Aker Drake was now on a 120 yard square island between the southern Ciedras Village Island and the mainland. No islet remains today. However there is a coral shoal where it may have been. Charts correctly depict the presence of mangroves. The Indians may have stripped the mangrove island for firewood, which contributed towards the mud being washed away and the island's disappearance. If this islet was always uninhabitable, Aker's choice is the southern Ciedras Village Island. It falls within the same parameters of identification. Aker continues by writing that a test should be conducted on the island for traces of the fort and its trench. This positioning is at odds with Dean Webster, who purports the three to four acre island of Corazón de Jesús, which lies 750 yards off the mainland. The difference in location arises from which point one measures, *the five leagues from the Cativaas.* Aker scribed an arc five leagues from Cativas Headland. The arc showed that the Ciedras Islets were sufficiently near that distance, close to a river and four cables from the shore. Webster traced his arc from the easternmost Holandes Keys, which he calls the Cativas. His arc strikes the coast slightly east of the Diablo river and the islet called Corazón de Jesús. He claims that no other island better matches the three criteria of area, distance from the mainland and distance from the Cativas. Here, he continues, is one of the best protected anchorages between Isla Pinos and Point San Blas and compared to Mr Aker's theory is, *"a better and more protected anchorage for Drake's five craft."* [The Webster Letters, 27.6.91.] Alternatively Aker's Ciedras Village could be described as being more towards *the bottome of the Bay*, if we consider the Gulf of San Blas as the Bay. Ciedras village is further off the shipping routes and is surrounded by more *shoales and sandy Ilands.*

On the aforementioned 1785 Spanish map published in his *The Defence of Portobelo* one sees the entire group of islands to the east of Point San Blas as being called the Cabezas or Cativas. Because they comprise at least forty-six islets, Drake's

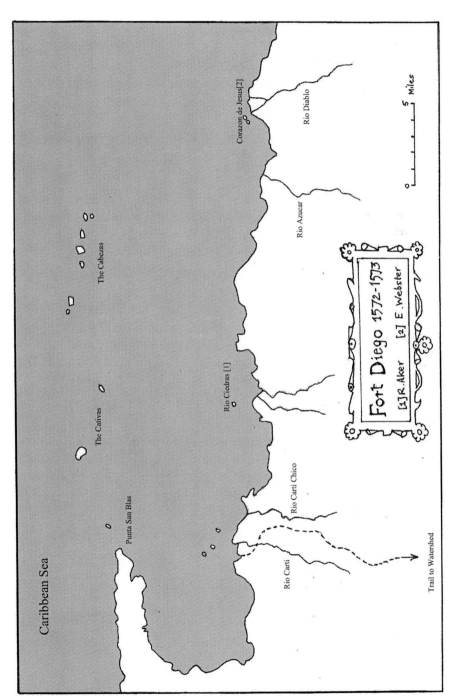

Caribbean Sea

Punta San Blas

The Cativas

The Cabezas

Rio Ciedras [1]

Corazon de Jesus[2]

Rio Azucar

Rio Diablo

Rio Carti

Rio Carti Chico

Trail to Watershed

Fort Diego 1572-1573

[1] R. Aker   [2] E. Webster

5 Miles

chroniclers could have worked from some sort of singular landmark and this could be Point Cativas, which is now called Point San Blas. Drake's subsequent movements will indicate which of the two theories of identification is correct.

On the 23 September, the first band of *cimarrones*, along with twelve others who had descended from the mountains, appeared on the shore and were ferried over to Drake's new headquarters. The alliance, which was to be so beneficial, was now finally cemented. The *cimarrones* were only too pleased to help Drake rob the Spaniards. Drake was informed that no treasure would be moved across the isthmus until after the rainy season. Therefore he had five months to wait.

The first time-consuming project was to use this strategic maritime setting for the building of a fortified base. To the dense virgin rain forest Drake sent, *"...his Pinnaces to the maine, to bring over great trees to make a Fort upon the same Iland,.."* [D.R. 281] The guns from the *Pasha* were taken ashore to arm the stockade, which was triangular in shape, so that its points faced the lie of the land and possible line of attack. Thus the apex faced just off to seaward. The walls were of timber and earth. The subsequent trench in front of the walls, made them thirteen feet in height. Both the Aker and Webster islets merited a triangle-wise fort. Inside the stockade the *cimarrones* had built two large huts of branches and palm leaves. Today the islanders construct their houses in the same fashion.

"Spurkite Iland"

On 7 October Francis took three pinnaces to Cartagena, whilst commanding his brother John, to complete the fort. His orders included going to the Cativas, where Francis had run ashore a ship which he had captured at the *Rio Grande*. Its planking would admirably serve the construction of gun platforms. Both men left the island that day. Francis sailed east and, *"That night wee came to an Ile, which hee called Spurkite Iland, because we found there great store of such a kinde a bird in shape, but verie delicate, of which wee killed and roasted many, staying there till the next day mid-noone when we departed thence."* [D.R. 282]

Initially to identify this island with certainty seemed a daunting task. I once again turned to Mr Aker who wrote, *"This is more than likely Puyadas Island 9^0 28½'N, 78^0 31' W. This name derives from the Spanish word for spike...the island lies in Man-of-War Keys. Man-of-War is another name for the frigate bird, which is probably what Drake found in abundance on the island. The bird is quite large, the size of a hen, with extremely long slender wings which may reach 7½ feet, and with a scissor-like tail. The island is probably a nesting colony."* [The Aker Letters, op. cit. 21.1.91.]

I saw such birds which were black with pointed wing tips. They spent the day feeding in the coastal mangroves and returned to the island for the night. Their few numbers in the dimming light ensured that they remained beyond the lens. However the following year albeit on the mainland, I was able to photograph frigate birds in flight but their spiked tails appeared shorter.

Puyadas Island is nineteen miles east of Aker's "Fort Diego" on Ciedras Island and, if Drake was making four knots, this was around five hours sailing and thus reachable on the same day. Puyadas lies only six miles away from Webster's "Fort Diego" on Corazón de Jesús, which is too close for a stopover.

Puyadas is nearly one mile long, sandy and shaded by coconut palms. Refreshing water is obtained from shallow pits. Like Drake I spent the night on the beach. A thin sleeping bag provided ample warmth. Comfort in the soft sand was assured by the absence of mosquitoes. The ants were the only slight irritant.

The sailing time to the next anchorage not only consolidates the identification of Puyadas as *Spurkite Iland* but working backwards, also subscribes to Mr Aker's theory in locating Drake's *Fort Diego.*

"a big Iland"

Around four hours after leaving Spurkite on the 8th at, *"about foure a clocke recovered a big Iland in our way, where we stayed all night, by reason that there was great store of fish, and especially of a great kind of shell-fish of a foot long. We called them Whelks."* [ibid] which I was lucky enough to encounter but on another island.

As far as Puyadas the sea was mirror smooth because of the presence of numerous islets. Frequently one could observe ten islets simultaneously. From here eastwards it was open sea to any island, which was on Drake's route to Cartagena and this was out of sight. I perceived the boatman's sense of unease as we were to traverse open sea and sail beyond the visual stretch of islands, which were his home. Initially, he refused to go any further. I dreaded the thought of coming all this way, realising that the omission of the next anchorage would make next year's return visit much more complicated. In a loud, firm and determined voice, I threatened not to pay his boss and quietly informed him that I would give him a tip.

After receiving encouragement from the resident family on Puyadas, we sailed forth. For the first time I found myself navigating by chart and compass. I was thrilled, when the base line arrow on the compass housing was pointing to the emerging hazy shape of the island.

In an attempt to reconfirm that Puyadas is Drake's *Spurkite Iland*, there is an island sixteen miles to the east, which with the easterly current, would have taken Drake the stated time to reach. Out in this eager sea our speed was now reduced from seven to five knots, making our journey three hours. To give some idea of the strength of this current, our return time to Puyadas was forty-five minutes longer.

This *big Iland* is **Cayo Ratones** at 9^0 22' N, 78^0 16' W. It is situated at the NW end of a group of minute keys, all of which lie three miles offshore. The only problem is that the island is not really *big* but only four cables long. However, since very few of the San Blas Islands are larger, this island could be considered *big* by comparison.

"The next morning we were cleere of these Ilands and Shoales, and haled off into the Sea." [D.R. 283]

This statement indicates that the *big Iland* is the isolated Cayo Ratones and is the most direct point of departure for Cartagena. By sailing Drake's route in the typical sea conditions with an awareness of time and distance it gave me a greater "feel" in reconstructing his course with the most accurate plotting of the islands. Consequently I was able to work back from Drake's departure from the last island to the two stated positions of *Fort Diego*.

The scenery on Ratones replicated all the other islands. Touring the archipelago was an escape from much of the 20th century. One is surrounded by a sparsely inhabited, typical tropical paradise of sandy, palm islands. The white beaches were enhanced by the bright, fierce sunlight. The sea created a kaleidoscope of colours, which ranged from transparent turquoise over the coral shallows to a cobalt blue spanning the expansive depths. Such environmental beauty was as usual not conveyed by the 16th century chronologist.

The Webster theory is best represented in his own words. *"The big island may be Nestupa near Alligandi, about 40 miles from Nargana. It is the largest they would have met and is the most likely place to set a course from the coast to the St. Bernards and Tolu. Spurkite is harder to determine solely from a map, though it took only four hours from there to reach the big island. However, several islets meet that criterion. Looking for a rookery, as you did, is a good idea, though this may be seasonal and, of course, could have changed over the centuries."* [The Webster Maps]

Webster's work is of such substance that it required field study. On sailing along the entire San Blas archipelago I searched in vain for another *big Iland*, which may have served as a landmark for a departure from the Panamanian coast. Nestupa is not a *big Iland* as Webster's map depicted. The coast is all rock and is surrounded by rocky shallows. A nearby island had been levelled by an earthquake earlier this century. Hence rigorous geographical changes may have diminished the sizes of some islands. My conclusion so far leans towards Mr Aker's identification.

San Bernados Islands, Colombia

"...neere the Ilands of Saint Bernards, wee chased two Frigates a shore and, recovering one of the Ilands, made our abode there some two dayes, to wash our Pinnaces and rake of the fish. Oct. 14-15" [D.R. 282]

The archipelago consists of ten islands and the exact beach is difficult to ascertain, although their number is few. During my second excursion, we visited the group's principal beaches on **La Palma** and **Mucura**. On the eastern end of the former a finger of white sand and coral protrudes a distance of 200 metres. This is the longest beach in the archipelago. The beach on Mucura is about fifty metres long, which is typical. The pinnaces would have been washed with salt water under the relentless blazing sun.

Tolú

"Oct. 16. Thence wee went towards Tolou and that day landed neere the Towne in a garden, where wee found certaine Indians, who...gathered for us such fruit as the Garden did yeeld, being many sorts of daintie fruits and roots,.." [ibid]

Today Tolú is a rustic, tranquil and picturesque village. The beach is of yellow sand, which is still backed by gardens. Within a few score metres one can pick bananas, coconuts and mangoes. The gardens are now divided and protected by barbed wire with branches used as posts.

Cartagena

"Oct. 16. Hence we departed presently, and rowed towards Charesha the Iland of Carthagene, and entred in at Boca Chica...wee sailed in towardes the Citie, and let fall our Grappers betwixt the Iland and the maine, right over against the goodly Garden Iland in which our Captain would not suffer us to land,.." [D.R. 283]

This refers to the orchards on the north shore of Tierra Bomba, being the south bank of the three-quarters of a mile wide Boca Grande entrance. Drake's reluctance to land proved well founded because their presence had been detected. A volley of 100 shot was fired at them by Spanish troops, that were on the north bank. This was at the southerly end of the peninsula, upon which Cartagena was built. The Spaniards were about two and a half miles from the town.

That night Drake departed seaward. The next day, 17 October, *"some two leagues off the harbour, wee tooke a barke,.."* [ibid] The haul of ammunition and provisions once again ensured Drake's continued survival, until he could return home rich. The next day the passengers were sent ashore. Taking the bark Drake anchored, *"in the mouth of Carthagene Harbour,.."* [ibid] That afternoon Spanish horsemen came down to Hicacos Point with a flag of truce promising Drake no harm and a supply of provisions that night. None arrived and by sunrise Drake perceived that the truce was designed to stall his departure so that the Spaniards could muster a force to capture him.

"...wee put to Sea to the Westward of the Iland, some three leagues off, where we lay at Hull the rest of the day and night. The next day, Oct. 20 in the afternoon..." Drake captured two frigates from Cartagena bound for Santo Domingo. *"...we tooke them within a league of the Towne, and came to anchor with them within Saker shot of the East Bulwarke."* The crew were now put ashore. *"The next morning, Oct. 21...they came downe to the Wester Point with a flag of truce,.."* Drake rowed ashore in a pinnace. *"When we were within a Cables length of the shoare the Spaniards fled, hiding themselves in the Woods, as being afraid of our Ordnance; but indeed to draw us on to land confidently, and to presume of our strength. Our Captaine commanding the Grapnell to be cast out of the sterne, veered the Pinnace a shoare, and as soone as shee touched the sand, hee alone leapt a shoare in their sight, to declare that hee durst set his foot a land,.."* [D.R. 284]

This landing was a symbol of Drake's defiance towards Spanish sovereignty. He immediately re-embarked, so that the Spaniards would not realise just how small his force was. *"They presently came forth upon the sand,.."* [ibid] A youth swam out to Drake with a message from the governor asking what the English wanted. Drake stated his desire for trade. All day was spent waiting for a more positive response. The night was passed watchfully aboard the captured frigates. The next morning Drake prevented the Spaniards from trying to retake their two ships. The Spaniards were repelled. Drake then burnt the vessels and repulsed further attacks because he was not able to leave the harbour for four days due to storms. On the fifth day, the 27th, Drake chased an approaching frigate. To avoid capture it ran ashore. Drake's pursuit was rebuffed by about 100 troops firing from Hicacos Point. One of Drake's great shot forced the Spaniards to retire to the woods, which Drake realised provided good cover for the snipers. The risks were too great, so once again the English withdrew.

These episodes occurred in Boca Grande and the SW and SE ends of the peninsula of Boca Grande. No woods remain because the whole peninsula, with its fine sandy beaches is now a popular tourist resort. Despite the trappings of the 20th century, the stunning topography of Cartagena harbour enables a visual reconstruction to be composed.

"...we concluded to go to sea againe, putting forth through Boca Chica, with intent to take downe our Masts,..to ride under the Rockes called Las Serenas, which are two leagues off at sea, as we had usually done aforetime, so that they could not discerne us from the Rocks." [D.R. 287]

This refers to the coral outcrops that form the **Rosario Islands**. Bad weather again, prevented a departure. For six days Drake rode out the gales and rain in the outer harbour. Boredom was interrupted by staving off a water-borne attack.

"Rio Grande" de la Magdalena

The westerly wind abated but prevented a return to Panamá. On 3 November Drake ran eastwards to the *Rio Grande* store houses. He arrived two days later and found them deserted.

Even the cattle had been driven into the mountains in an attempt to starve him away. Drake was low on victuals, due to spoilage by the rain at Cartagena and rough seas. En route to Santa Marta, a frigate was boarded but it only yielded disappointment.

Santa Marta

Drake entered the port, *"...upon hope to finde some shipping in the Road, or Limpets on the rockes, or succour against the storme in that good Harbour. Being arrived and seeing no shipping, wee anchored under the Wester point, where is high land, and, as wee thought, free in safetie from the Towne, which is in the bottome of the Bay,.."* [D.R. 288-9]

Drake was now under the NW cliffs that afford the haven much of its protection. The point is covered with cactus and shrubs. The intermittent absence of vegetation on the cliff face, enables the speckles of white rock to give the point a conspicuous appearance. The gentle swell enabled my boatman to manoeuvre close to the rocks, which were still profusely carpeted with limpets. Drake was within half a mile of the town and was immediately observed. The Spaniards conveyed cannons to the cliff top and drove him off.

"East of Santa Marta"

Three leagues eastward a ship was boarded whose cargo rescued Drake and his men from the verge of starvation. Here for twenty-two miles the green Sierra Madre sink abruptly into the deep and blue seething sea as it swirls around the rocky headlands, which guard ten beautiful remote coves.

On the 13th Drake, *"sent in Edward Hixom...to search out some Harbour along the Coast, who, having found out a little one, some ten or twelve leagues to the East of Santa Martha, where in sounding he had good and sufficient water, presently returned, and our Captain brought in his new Prize."* [D.R. 290]

The Spaniards were released in exchange for helping Drake to find water and provisions. A few Indians augmented Drake's supplies. They were governed by a Spaniard, who lived in a town nearly three miles away. Drake left that evening.

To my horror all I saw at twenty to twenty five nautical-miles east of Santa Marta were long beaches being battered by crashing surf! I returned to Santa Marta for a re-think. As Drake's pinnaces had been plying up and down through the night after capturing the ship some nine miles east of Santa Marta, the distance to this cove must have been over exaggerated. On Christmas Day in 1986 I hired a boat from nearby Rodadero and conducted a survey, based somewhat upon a process of elimination. From a map I favoured the penultimate cove of Ancón Cinto. Although it was closer to the stated distance, it was still only half way. Except for the last cove it was smaller than the others. Unlike the other coves there was an old Indian trail leading inland that skirted the adjacent cove to the west. This was feasibly the route of communication between the governing Spaniard and the Indians in the harbour.

The sea is tranquil but suddenly pounds on to the yellow sand, because it abruptly shallows within twenty metres of the shore. The beach is backed by coconut palms, adjacent to which is a river. Through dense woodland four streams also flow into the cove. Apart from two houses the cove is uninhabited. Its dimensions are two kilometres long by one kilometre wide and it is one of the most beautiful places in the world. The other coves are equally enchanting.

Upon returning home my Colombian friend sent me a more detailed map of the harbours, which form the Tairona National Park. I felt niggled for not having examined the last sizeable harbour. Three years later to the day, I returned to find that it was unsuitable, because it was too rough. I am convinced that Ancón Cinto is most likely the harbour. Because Drake's stay was short and mundane, it has always been omitted by Drake's biographers. Consequently hitherto, no attempt has been made to assert its whereabouts.

San Bernados Islands

En route back to his base in Panamá, *"On Nov. 22...we came to Saint Bernards, where we staided many houres, finding but twelve Botijos of wine, of all the store wee left, which had escaped the curious search of the Enemy (who had beene there) for they were very deepe in the ground."* [D.R. 291]

Although the exact beach or beaches to which Drake's sojourns refer cannot be positively identified, my two excursions have enabled the scenery to document vividly Drake's contact. Furthermore I was pleased to photograph five Spanish wine jars in the museum at Old Panama City.

"Fort Diego"

On 27 November Drake arrived at his hideaway base camp. At first he was no doubt pleased that the fort had been completed. However he was grieved by the death of his brother along with that of Richard Allen. John Drake was returning to the fort with a pinnace loaded with the required planks, when a Spanish frigate was spotted. John wanted to impress Captain Francis by taking this prize, in spite of being poorly armed. All they could muster were a broken pointed sword, a fish spear and a caliver. John boarded with the sword and used a pillow as a shield. The Spaniards were well armed and discharged their muskets to repel John Drake's foolhardy and fatal attempt.

Francis was executor of John's will. The will reveals that John left a widow named Alice, who would benefit from the profits of the voyage. Prior to embarking upon this expedition I had been enthused by Mr Aker's idea of excavating the islet for the remains of the timber stockade and the graves. However the islets of Ciedras and Corazón de Jesús are densely populated and would present problems.

The Spanish fleet was expected within the next two months. In order not to keep the Spaniards on a high state of alert Drake remained ashore to give the impression that he had left for home. Much time was spent in the forest hunting *hogs*, *pheasants* and *guanas*. The New Year witnessed another tragedy. Many of Drake's force were killed, possibly by yellow fever. This was attributed to drinking brackish water, because water was not taken far enough up one of the rivers.

During my three day canoe excursion and during the following Easter, I penetrated all the rivers near both "Fort Diegos". I found the water was sweet from 500 metres up-river. On 3 January Drake suffered a further misfortune, when his other brother Joseph died in his arms. So that the disease could be better understood, Drake ordered an autopsy to be carried out on Joseph. The surgeon, who had recovered from this disease, found Joseph's liver swollen, the heart sodden and his intestines yellow. Ironically the surgeon died four days later, as a result of accidentally poisoning himself with his own experimental potions. Drake's depleted force was reduced to about thirty from an original complement of seventy-three.

Meanwhile the *cimarrones* were combing the countryside to glean intelligence with regard to the expected arrival of the treasure fleet, which they soon reported had docked at Nombre de Dios. On 30 January, Drake dispatched the *Lion* to the seamost island of the Cativas. A captured frigate from Tolú to Nombre de Dios confirmed the news. To keep Drake's presence a secret the one woman and twelve man crew were held prisoner aboard the *Pasha*, which was hauled ashore on *Fort Diego*, now called *Slaughter Iland* on the account of twenty-eight deaths. Drake was now in conference with the *cimarrones* preparing for a great and long journey across the isthmus towards Panama City in pursuit of the treasure-laden mule trains. It was a journey that was to reverberate through the annals of English history.

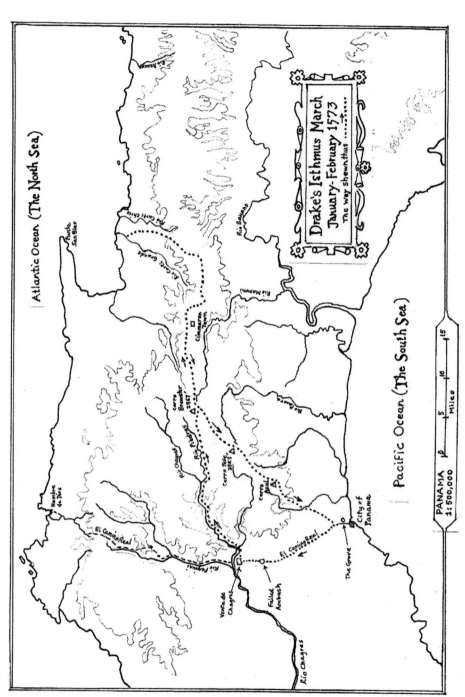

Atlantic Ocean (The North Sea)

Pacific Ocean (The South Sea)

Drake's Isthmus March
January-February 1573
The way shewn thus ·········

Punta
San Blas

Nombre
de Dios

El Camino Real

Cinnamen
Town

Cerro Brewster
2967

Rio Pequeni

Rio Chagres

Cerro Tigre
3353

Cerro Azul
3353

El Camino Real

Venta de
Chagres

Failed
Ambush

The Grove

City of
Panama

Rio Chagres

Rio Pequeni

Rio Mandinga

Rio Bayano

PANAMA
1:500,000

0   5   10   15
Miles

150

The Isthmus March

Ellis Hixom was left in charge of the fort, with about six men to guard the prisoners. He was told not to trust any messenger unless he carried Drake's own handwriting. With a great store of shoes packed the eighteen English, accompanied by thirty *cimarron* guides and porters departed on 3 February. However, according to the subsequent contemporary Spanish letters and reports, Drake must have set-off during the middle of January because they record the attack on *Venta de Chagres* as being on the 29 or 31 of January. This means that there was a discrepancy of around two weeks. This can be attributed to the fact that *Drake Revived* was written two decades after the events from the memories of some of Drake's companions. Logs and other records may have been used. Unless stated otherwise dates are taken from *Drake Revived*.

The trek could have begun from the adjacent mainland, which would be at the river. It has proved impossible to reconstruct the route march with definite accuracy. What follows lends some weight to the Webster theory. Dean Edwin Webster is the only person in the world to have made a serious, commendable attempt.

"Fort Diego is no doubt so named because it lay near the mouth of the Rio Diego. As you know, the terrain in crossing the isthmus is exceedingly rugged. Perhaps the best route (at least the one in use at the beginning of this century) runs up the Rio Diablo (Rio Diego) to a pass that opens onto the Pacific slope. It would have been an important river to the cimarrones and a likely place to maintain contact with them. Up it also

Drake would have been guided in his trip across the isthmus."
[The Webster Letters, 27.6.91.]

Each day's journey began at sunrise, which from my
observation, was at 6am. Four *cimarrones* would march one
mile in advance of the column to clear a passage. Twelve
cimarrones acted as vanguard and another twelve performed as
rearguard. The *cimarron* chiefs marched in the middle with the
English. For their security all walked in silence. From ten
o'clock there was a two hour blissful rest at a river, where
prolonged immersion helped to alleviate the discomfort of
excessive sweating, which lessened with increased altitude.
The march resumed until four o'clock, being three hours before
darkness. The night was spent free from any unseasonable
shower in thatched huts impromptu built by the *cimarrones*, or
in huts previously erected along their well-established hidden
trails. The food included roasted *plantains*, a wide range of
fruits and swine - all supplied by the *cimarrones* in their
attempts to comfort their weary-footed English friends.

On the third day, the expedition arrived at a *cimarron Towne*
that was, *"...seated neere a faire river, on the side of a hill,
environed with a dike of eight foot broad and a thicke mud wall
of ten foot high,..It had one long and broad street lying East
and West, and two other crosse streets of lesse bredth and
length. There were in it some five or six and fiftie
households,..This Towne is distant thirtie five leagues from
Nombre de Dios, and fortie five from Panama."* [D.R. 298]

These distances are nautical leagues and are wildly too far to
the east. If they were equated to the Spanish land league, then
the camp could have been inland, midway between Webster's

and Aker's "Fort Diego's". Webster writes that the exact site of the town is unknown but speculates that it was probably on the Jicoteca or a neighbouring tributary of the Bayano or perhaps the Tabardi. Four hundred years of torrential rains would have levelled the earthwork but not all of the lateral strategic sculpturing.

The party left the next day at noon, which *Drake Revived* states was on the 7 February. The next few days travel would take them through the Bayano valley and into the hills above Chepo. Here lived a tribe of hispanicized Indians. Drake would have kept well to the north to maintain the element of surprise. *"If the route taken by the later Spanish trail was followed it would have been necessary to depart from it before the Bayano turns south. They could have either cut to the upper Mamoni or taken a ridge trail between it and the Corpus Cristi."*
[The Webster Essays, Drake in Panamá: A Geography]

Ten miles east of Chepo a dirt-stone trail leads to the Caribbean coast near the Rio Cartí Grande. By following this road Drake's footsteps would definitely be intersected. John and I hired a taxi out of Panama City. The steep and rutted trail soon stopped the vehicle in its tracks. Delving into the depths of my mental resources, I approached drivers of pick-up trucks in the nearby village of La Loma for assistance. For $20 we were driven to the radio mast. This confirmed we were at the highest point, which the map states as 520 metres.

Drake would have wanted to march the shortest route over such rugged terrain. I now believe that he would have sailed as far west as possible and ascended the Cartí trail. This trail would have saved a gruelling twenty-six miles. The red mud Cartí trail is the only trail, along which one can reach the watershed of the isthmus by jeep. Through the influential offices of René Gómez, British Motors of Panama City, provided gratis, John and I, with a Land Rover for the day. We remembered the previous journey to the watershed. However the descent to the Caribbean became very narrow, rutted and steep. Recent light rain had already created such soft mud, that GPS six miles short of the mouth of the Cartí all hope was abandoned. Here was a dangerous steep drop immediately on the east side of the trail: this was the upper reaches of the Rio Cartí Chico. A Cuna Indian, rightly informed us, that only in February was through passage guaranteed. However we did experience the jungle scenery, over-hanging the three metres wide, ancient Indian trail.

Previously on the ridge, John and I, had sampled walking west along a short, cool and shady jungle trail. From here on Webster's and Aker's interpretations of the route as far as Venta de Chagre are similar.

The English were now about three thousand feet up in the cool mountain air. *"All the way was thorow woods very coole and pleasant, by reason of those goodly and high Trees that grow there so thicke that it is cooler travelling there under them in that hot region, then it is in the most parts of England in the Summer time. This gave a speciall encouragement unto us all, that we understood there was a great Tree about the midway, from which we might at once discerne the North sea from whence we came, and the South sea whether we were going."* *The fourth day following we came to the height of the desired Hill (a very high Hill, lying East and West, like a ridge betweene the two Seas)..."* [D.R. 299]

"For much of their journey high ridges on both sides of the Bayano Valley precluded such a sighting. Below the junction of the Bayano and the Palantal the southern ridge falls away, making it possible at certain five hundred meter points along the Cordillera de San Blas to see both oceans. Here however, the ridge line is too broken to have been the route of the march. North of the Mamoni River, the Cordillera drops a little above three hundred meters. At six hundred meter points along the Mamoni-Corpus Cristi and Mamoni-Pacora ridge (Montanuelas de Tapagra) such a view is again possible. There is today an east-west trail along the upper Mamoni which turns south to the Montanuelas de Tapagra, then west following their peaks. From the highest of these it is about sixty-four kilometers (fourteen leagues) as the crow flies to the Jicoteca a hard four days' journey in such country." [Webster, ibid]

Cerro Brewster

Pedro, the chief *cimarron*, beckoned Drake to follow him up the *"great high Tree, in which they had made divers steps to ascend up neere unto the top, where they had made a convenient Bower wherein tenne or twelve men might easily sit: and from thence we might without any difficulty plainly see th' Atlantick Ocean whence now we came and to the south Atlanticke so much desired. South and North of this Tree they had felled certaine Trees that the prospect might be cleerer,.."* [D.R. 300]

It was one of Panama's clearer days, when the clouds that normally envelop the Cordillera were fewer. This was during the dry season. To replicate such a clear view one has to avoid mid-February onwards, when the dry jungle is subjected to slash and burn. Consequently particles from the burning and the wind-blown dry soil from the cleared ground fill the air to obscure the view. In the rainy season the cloud cover is too dense.

Drake was experiencing one of the most spiritual moments of his life. He prayed that God would grant him the honour of sailing into the fabled Pacific, from where much of Spain's riches began their journey. Consequently the seeds of thought for a world voyage were now being sown. All Drake's men studied this, one of the world's most unusual views. John Oxenham stated that he would try and reach the Pacific before Drake. Oxenham did become the first Englishman to sail on the Pacific but was captured by the Spaniards and taken to Lima. It was a cruel irony that when Drake was in Lima harbour and so far from England, that Oxenham should be only six miles away awaiting execution.

"After the sighting, Drake could have continued westward parallel to the upper Pacora, turning south between the slopes of Cerro Tubova and the upper Utive to the savannas. Such a route would correspond to their, [Webster, ibid] *ordinary march through woods yet two days more as before without any great varietie."* [D.R. 300]

This area can be reached by a gravel road that penetrates twelve miles beyond Cerro Azul. In 1992 once again I landed in Panamá at dawn and was eager to begin *Drake-ing* immediately. This attitude helps reduce the long term costs. The more I can cram into an expedition the sooner the project is finished. A conventional taxi was too expensive. As I walked, carrying the rucksack, I knew I would attract the part-time freelance drivers. Soon I was with a man, who besides being a carpenter used his car to earn extra money. I was eighteen miles inland being five miles past Cerro Azul and still the slash and burn had robbed the mountains of their natural foliage. Although I was on a descending ridge that Drake may have used, or at worst three kilometres off his route, I was not to flavour the scenery that faced Francis Drake. I had to settle for the configuration of the terrain. Just before catching the plane home in 1993, René Gómez took me to the highest point, being Cerro Jefe, that was a few miles further inland. The early morning sky was clear. The view over the jungle canopy with pockets of minute cloud lingering over the shorter trees was unforgettable but had to be consigned to memory because my film supply was exhausted!

The dense canopy of the forest gave way to open country. *"But then we came to march in a Champion Country, where the grasse groweth not only in great length as the knotgrasse groweth in many places, but to such height that the inhabitants are faine to burne it thrise in the yeere that it may bee able to feede their Cattle, of which they have thousands. For it is a kinde of grasse with a stalke as big as a great wheaten reed, which hath a blade issuing from the top of it, on which though the cattle feed yet it groweth every day higher, untill the top be too high for an Oxe to reach."* [ibid]

The visitor can easily view this *Champion Country* from Cerro Azul. From here, Drake would have had his first view of Panama City. The modern road traverses the undulating grassy landscape and the ridge, from which Drake saw the two oceans, is clearly visible. In the wet season of August 1983 I was lucky

enough to creep up on the timid cattle using the cover of bushes. I captured a picture of the described grass stalk adjacent to a cow's mouth. However Drake must have seen another breed of cattle because today, as in Colombia, one sees cattle egret, which is a 19th century immigrant from Africa. To my surprised disappointment the spikelets at the top of the grass are not evident towards the end of the dry season, when I had hoped to create a stock of spare slides. My three visits to this area produced pictures depicting a wet, lush green, to a dried-out paler shade of green at the end of the dry season. Colour-wise Drake would have seen the in-between shades of green.

"In these three last dayes march in the Champion, as we past over the hilles we might see Panama five or sixe times a day, and the last day we saw the Ships riding in the roade." [D.R. 301]

In August 1983, I had neglected to include this panorama, which would not have been so clear as Drake's dry season view. Even under the blue skies of March, there was a haze from the slash and burn. However, the descending rolling hills with the suburbs of Panama City, enveloping Panamá Viejo, (Old Panamá) backed by the Pacific Ocean, provided an encapsulating and worthwhile view.

"The grove"

For Drake and his men the scarcity of trees greatly increased their physical discomforts. Within a day's march of Panamá the party had to walk stealthily following the curve of the hills, northwards of the open trails to avoid the hunters and fowlers from the city. Their immediate destination was a grove, being a safe place to rest, *"lying within a league of Panama, where wee might lie safely undiscovered ...alongst a certaine River which at that time was almost dryed up...and...neare the high way that leadeth from thence to Nombre de Dios."* [ibid] The grove was east of the Camino Real. On the world voyage, Drake told his prisoner Nicolas Jorge that the *cimarrones* had taken him to the mangroves near the garden of María Alvarez on the outskirts of Panamá, from where he had seen the Royal Houses. Mangroves exist at the head of the cove on the NE side of the old city.

Drake arrived at 3 o' clock when, *"...our Captaine did behold and view the most of all that faire Citie, discerning the large streete which lieth directly from the sea into the land, South and North."* [D.R. 302] The city was founded on 15 August 1519 by the famous conquistador Pedrarias Dávila. It was the oldest Spanish settlement on the Pacific. The developing city contained 400 substantially built wooden houses. The resident and transient population were 500 and 800 respectively. Most of the inhabitants originated from Andalusía, Spain.

At the stated distance from Old Panamá are hills, that afford excellent views of the ruined city. Urbanisation has destroyed any presence of the rivulet and is demolishing "Drake's Hill". In March 1999 I returned just in time, to the same spot, to improve upon the dull, rainy season picture that I had taken in 1983. Drake must have stood on this southerly extremity for the closest view. By GPS he was .6 of a mile from the city square. The position of the aforementioned road remains. It cuts through the remaining hillocks, as it runs between the ruined stoned buildings. They include a cathedral tower and the Santo Domingo Convent. The latter was founded in 1571. Furthermore to embellish the historical atmosphere, there is the well preserved stone King's Bridge, that spans the Rio Abajo and over its cobbles clattered the hoofs of the treasure-laden mules. In Drake's day the bridge was of wood.

The Camino Real

Around 5.30pm a *cimarron* was sent into the city to discover what night the next mule train was to leave for Nombre de Dios. They left at sunset to avoid crossing the open savannah or *champion* country during the heat of day. Once in the jungle the mules travelled by day and could cover the fifty miles between two and four days. The *cimarron* returned with information that the Treasurer of Lima was to leave that night with fourteen mules. Eight were to carry gold and one jewels. There were two other trains of fifty mules, each carrying provisions and some silver. Immediately, Drake hastily marched four leagues along this Royal Road to lay his ambush.

Dean Edwin Webster noted that urban development had obliterated all traces of the trail for the first eight miles. Webster cites two maps which depict this stretch of the original route. Between three and five kilometres north of **María**

Henríquez he found a few post-Drake paved sections. John and I arrived here by taxi from Panama City. Around fifty metres west of the highway I found the first portion, along which John located the best collection cobble stones. These were frequently interspersed with shrubs and low trees. Three hundred metres further north we both climbed the roadside fence but it was John, who discovered a short section of large stones. The cutting of the modern road and the fencing had at least, destroyed the edge of the Camino, along which Drake had hastily marched. Webster's map from the 1970s had re-emphasised that we were following Drake's footsteps by naming this trail, *Old Spanish trail.*

Theoretically, it was in the northern environs of the present-day village of **Calzada Larga**, where the ambush was set, being within two leagues of *Venta de Chagres*. Webster had informed me that the trail crossed the modern road and then passed east of the cemetery. In the vicinity of the main road nobody knew of the trail's existence! I asked a grave digger in the cemetery for help. He led us south along the trail back to the main road. We walked along an excellent cobbled section. John lifted the vegetation, either side of where people trod, to discover that the original width was about twelve feet, as stated in *Drake Revived.* [306] We drank much needed water at a house at the side of the trail just off the main road. The lady was unaware that many thousands of tons of treasure once passed her doorstep!

The force was divided in half and was hidden fifty paces either side of the trail in long grass. To avoid accidentally killing each other and, so that all the mules could be pulled to the ground by their heads, the two parties were staggered. Drake was to rush the front half of the train and Oxenham the rear. Within an hour, in the still of night, the sweet sound of the mule bells was heard both from the direction of *Venta de Chagres* and Panamá. The former train of less valuable goods was to be allowed to pass.

However Robert Pike, under the excessive influence of wine, tried to approach this mule train and, despite being smothered by a *cimarron*, was seen by an outrider. Drake was not aware of this incident but, due to the hardness of the ground, clearly discerned a horse's trot had turned into a gallop. Drake was hoping that the Spaniard may have become nervous, knowing that along this dark and dangerous trail the *cimarrones* had attacked the pack trains; and not on account of him being discovered. The rider warned the mule train from Panamá. Consequently the mules carrying the victuals were sent on ahead. Drake was foiled. The skirmish had only yielded two horse loads of silver. Despite conducting the most audacious raid to date upon Spanish-American treasure, Drake had to accept another set-back, which was the making of his own man! Drake must have felt quite desperate for he knew that within hours his futile raid would begin to alert every Spaniard on the Isthmus and his survival in the midst of the jungle was solely dependent on the *cimarrones*. In consultation with Pedro, Drake resolved not to retrace his long and exhausting journey but to take the shortest route back to his ships, which meant marching forwards into the clutches of his enemies.

After fortifying themselves from the captured provisions, Pedro renewed his commitment to Drake's cause, despite the pending increased danger and, using the mules, led Drake along the Camino towards *Venta de Chagres*. The mules were released within a mile of the settlement.

"There the way is cut thorow the Woods, about ten or twelve foote broade, so as two Recoes [recuas, is Spanish for mule trains.] *may passe one by another. The fruitfulnesse of the soyle causeth that with often shredding and ridding the way those Woods grow as thicke as our thickest hedges in England that are oftnest cut."* [D.R. 306]

Drake had fled northwards. At present-day Calzada Larga the trail divided and it was the west trail to *Venta de Chagres* that Webster noted was paved. Nonetheless we cannot be certain as to which divide Drake took.

In 1983 I tried to find the jungle trail in the region of the ambush. To my astonishment I encountered a well preserved section. In the middle of all this jungle I thought that I was walking exactly in Drake's footsteps during one of the most colourful events in his life. In places the cobble stones remained! Here typically the trail is about ten metres wide, and would have enabled two oncoming mule trains to pass side-by-side. In 1991 I inspected at least a half mile section that passed through varied terrain and flora. Generally the trail is engulfed by trees but in places and most refreshingly an expanse of blue sky caps acres of the eight feet high grass, which concealed Drake and his band of robbers. To the other extreme the trail becomes a narrow and steep ravine, over-hung by vines.

After reading Dean Webster's paper on the Camino Real, I realised that I had found the Cruces Trail. However my disappointment was tempered. In 1992 I flew low over Webster's documented route of the Camino. I sadly realised that since his observations the jungle along the entire route has virtually been destroyed. Since I had not found any trace of the Camino, I now savoured my photographic experience on the Cruces Trail, because it was the nearest remaining environmental comparison. My pilgrimage along the Cruces Trail made it apparent how Drake and his men were perpetually sheathed in dripping sweat, as they toiled relentlessly along the ankle-bending Camino, with their feet wearily crunching the dried carpet of leaves, which in places had not quite covered the occasional cluster of cobble stones, that studded the trail. Their discomfort was heightened by the flies pitching upon their numerous bleeding scratches which crisscrossed their sweaty dirty hands, which had occasionally come into contact with the coarsest of vegetation. There was never a breeze to temper the stifling heat but every step was closer to the hitherto elusive concept of riches. As I felt isolated, I deduced that if it were not for the Blacks, Drake may never have become rich. No wonder then, during his world voyage, he stated his life lasting affection for the *cimarrones*.

In 1993 I showed John Thrower the cobbled section. From his studies of Roman roads he was prompted to notice that, where the cobbles were at their lowest point, the engineers had cleverly built in a channel to drain off the rain to minimise the amount of puddles. This aspect of engineering was obviously applied to the Camino Real.

"Venta de Chagres"

A troop of soldiers accompanied by friars were encountered. They summoned the outlaws to identify themselves. Drake cried out that they were English, which in the name of the King, resulted in a demand for their surrender. Drake replied that for the queen's honour he must be given free passage. In the ensuing exchange of shot, John Harris was wounded and died the next day. When Drake realised that a rain shower had diminished the ferocity of the Spanish firing, he ordered a charge. The *cimarrones* overtook the English. One *cimarron* was run through with a pike but killed his assailant before dying. The Spaniards were routed and Drake's party ran into the way station of *Venta de Chagres*, which the English called *Venta Cruz*.

The town was the first rest stop for the recuas. It was up-river from Casa de Las Cruces and situated where the Camino fords the Chagres. The settlement was entered by a bridge. *"...the Guard which we set as well on the bridge which we were to pass over at the townes end where we entered (they have no other entrance into the towne by Land...)"* [D.R. 308-9] According to *Drake Revived* it comprised about fifty houses, a monastery and large strongly built warehouses, which stored goods being transported between Nombre de Dios and Panamá via the Chagres. Allowance must be made for exaggerating the number of buildings, since accuracy cannot be expected during a short period of intense pillaging, especially at night. Drake ordered that none of the women be molested and no Spaniard killed, unless armed. After nearly two hours Drake hastened towards the coast. Several days were spent marching on hungry stomachs, as time could not be spared to hunt for meat. En route Francis reiterated his determination to leave Panamá rich. However, even at this stage of Drake's activities, none of the Spanish dispatches mention him by name.

Due to the construction of the Panama Canal, a dam was built and the Chagres has flooded forming the Madden Lake. In 1983, I chose the trail and riverside village of Santa Rosa, six miles west to depict an environmentally acceptable scene. Nine years later I gladly learnt that the site of Drake's *Venta Cruz* was discovered by Webster in 1973.

At the end of this dry season, the level of the lake had fallen from the usual 220-250 feet to 201 feet. This exceptionally low

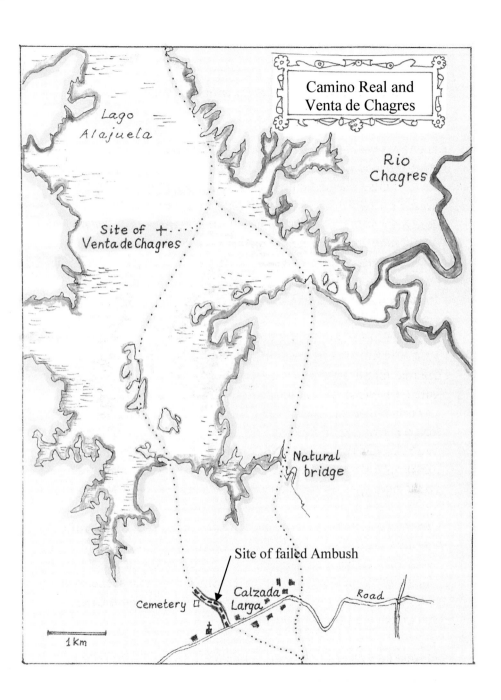

Camino Real and
Venta de Chagres

Lago
Alajuela

Rio
Chagres

Site of +
Venta de Chagres

Natural
bridge

Site of failed Ambush

Cemetery

Calzada
Larga

Road

1 Km

level also exposed several sections of the cobble-paved highway on the lake's east bank between the 200 and 220 feet level.

Webster observed, *"The Camino Real ran north along a ridge to the Rodríguez, then crossed it and the low land to its north toward a series of fords where the Chagres was split by two large gravel shoals...About 600 feet south of the point where the Camino Real drops to the Rodríguez a cobble path leads from a stone patio to the Camino, this may well have been a guardhouse at the town entrance."*
[The Webster Essays, The Site of Venta de Chagres]

Webster notes that the bridge could not have crossed the Chagres because seasonal flooding would have prevented its maintenance. Instead, if Drake had entered along the eastern trail, the bridge would have spanned the Quebrada Rodríguez. If he had marched along what was later to be the paved west road, the bridge would have crossed the Rio Chico Viejo. Webster determined the exact site of *Venta de Chagres* by the positioning of colonial artifacts. A heavy concentration were found along the Rodríguez ridge, extending NW to what was once a high bank, known today as Treasure Island that overlooks the river. Hence the settlement lay between the Rio Chico Viejo and the Quebrada Rodríguez at $9^0 14'$N. $79^0 34'$W.

To determine if a visit is worthwhile, one can verify the current water level with the Canal Hydrographic Office. The visitor can reach the vicinity of the exposed site by driving north from Calzada Larga to within easy walking distance. When my driver reached the end of the stony road, I was able to walk along the south bank of the Chagres to where it meets Lake Madden. I had plotted Webster's information on a current map. I deduced that due to the water level, I was two kilometres SE short of the site. Days later in the National Museum I saw pictures of Webster's team excavating the causeway. I felt tantalised because I had seen similar views but could not confirm that I had stood on the same patch of ground. The land bordering the lake is low. The latter is dotted with gravel islets. What I had at least accurately documented was the configuration of the surrounding hills.

A year later in 1993, René Gómez had indicated on a map where I could hire a boat on the scarcely populated shores of the lake. John and I chartered a dugout canoe from the village of Nuevo Vigía on the lake's west shore on a rainy afternoon. We reached a scattering of huts on the north shore of the Chagres, marked on the map as Tranquilla. The man who came to greet us had accommodated Dean Edwin Webster twenty years earlier during his field studies! With precision accuracy, he pointed to the flooded site of *Venta de Chagres*. Coupled with the boatman's knowledge, we navigated two kilometres WSW. John held the canoe against one of the many tree stumps which protrude from the lake. Through murky water I pulled myself about twenty feet down the trunk in an unsuccessful attempt to place my feet upon *Venta de charges*. Nonetheless I emerged gratified that I had physically been as close as possible to Drake's footsteps. The excitement continued.

Webster's former host had also directed us a kilometre to the NW, where a cobbled section of the Camino Real emerges from the inaccessible custody of the lake. A two metre wide trail of brownish stones lay intact for an uphill distance of about forty metres. It was quite possible that these were the same stones upon which Drake and his highwaymen had trampled in retreat from their abortive raids This was once again literally being in Drake's footsteps!

We are not given details of Drake's return route, except that he reached a river other than that from which he had set out. Webster has outlined a probable route.

"... follow the Chagres to the Rio Indio, then travel parallel to the Indio to the saddle between Cerro El Jefe and Cerro Tobora, crossing to meet their own trail near the Utive River. They would retrace their route as far as the Icanti, then go up its eastern tributary, the Aguas Claras, from which today an Indian trail crosses to the Rio Azucar. On its banks, just across the divide and three leagues from their ships, they would take their first rest." [Webster, A Geography, op. cit.]

"River Tortuga"

When Drake had returned to the Caribbean coast, he had walked at least 150 miles in nearly three weeks. The arrival at *Venta de Chagres* was near two weeks into the march. If we accept the Spanish accounts that either Thursday 29 or Saturday the 31 January as the date of the attack on *Venta de Chagres*, the trek to the coast would have taken just over a week. From Webster's interpretation of the route, Drake had arrived at the River Azucar, or in Aker's opinion the Cartí Grande. As stated earlier, I believe that Drake began his march here. Whichever river it was Drake was following its watercourse from the mountains to the sea.

"In our absence the rest of the Symerons had built a little Towne within three leagues off the port where our Ship lay." [D.R. 310]

The new village would be well up-river: not on the coast for fear of the Spaniards. The stated distance of three leagues would be from the village to the fort, via the estuary. The Cartí is by far the larger of the two and indeed ranks as the major river along Panama's north coast. By canoe I spent two hot stifling hours gliding up-river for over two miles. All the way the water course was deep, being at least thirty metres wide.

Upon arrival, which was the 22 February, Drake dispatched a *cimarron* along the shore to notify Ellis Hixom of his captain's return. Hixom could hear the Negro calling from the mainland. The message that Drake was to be collected at the river was proved genuine. Hixom was given a gold toothpick, upon which Drake had carved, "By me Francis Drake". The *cimarron* had guided Hixom by sea to the thirty metre wide estuary, which the *cimarrones* had called Tortuga.

"That after noone towards three a clocke wee were come downe to that River not past halfe an houre before we saw our Pinnace ready to receive us,.." [D.R. 311]

Unlike the Azucar estuary, which is lined by mangroves, at the Cartí Grande Drake's men could have waited on a yellow sandy beach, where they rested their sore feet, as each man was on his last pair of shoes. However *Drake Revived* makes no mention of a beach. This omission does not preclude that there was a beach. Despite the fact that the *cimarrones* had been porters and even carried sick and weary Englishmen, it had been an endurance test for our hardy ancestors. They had truly suffered, even by the standards of their time. This is difficult for us to appreciate in our age of technological comforts, unless one actually hikes along the Panamanian trails.

"Another River..."

Despite the happy reunion, the disappointment of returning without the gold was etched into every man's facial expressions. The assembly was not quite complete. Some of the men were not strong enough to walk from the new *cimarron* village to the estuary and the following day were collected from, *"...another River in the bottome of the Bay..."* [ibid]

On page 280 in Wright's publication of *Drake Revived* there is another reference to *the bottome of the Bay*. I interpret this as travelling west to the head of the bay, beyond a north to south line drawn between Point San Blas and the Rio Cartí Grande.

Referring to the Aker identification, this can only be the small River Cartí, the Cartí Chico, five miles closer to *Fort Diego*, where again there is a small beach. In Webster's view this river is 1½ miles nearer *Fort Diego*, SE of Azucar islet village. However, the river's closest beach is half a mile westward. This discussion is not too important because Drake was already most likely back on *Fort Diego*.

Both the Aker and Webster theories show the *River Tortuga* at the exact described distance from *Fort Diego*. The Cartí Grande and Azucar are about four miles from their respective *Fort Diego*, a distance that accords with *Drake Revived*.

Despite Webster's sterling study of the inland march, I favour the Aker positioning of *Fort Diego*. I reached a conclusive decision after conducting a survey of the alternative routes from a light plane. The terrain is exceptionally rugged, especially due to the numerous river valleys, which increase towards the east. If Drake were at Webster's *Fort Diego*, it would have saved at least an extra agonising day's march to have sailed the seventeen miles west to the Ciedras river to begin the ascent into the mountains. However photographically there is very little to distinguish between them.

"Fort Diego"

Drake informed his company that he would launch another attack on the mule trains. When the men had recovered their strength, Captain Francis reminded them that to keep morale high all must be kept busy. Opinions varied on how best to pass the interim time.

Veragua

Drake Revived gives no geographical clue to where the following events occurred. Verification has been obtained from the book, *Old Panama & Castillo del Oro* by Dr. Anderson. Dean Webster very kindly supplied me with the relevant photocopied pages.

From his former voyages Francis Drake had learnt of the modest gold deposits at *Llerena*, which bordered the Rio de Santiago del Turluri three leagues inland along a flat trail from the River Concepción in Veragua province. Mining had begun sometime after 1555 and was now at its peak. By the end of the century, production was in terminal decline. Some of the *cimarrones* had worked here as slaves and were prepared to guide Drake to the treasure house, which was located in the port of **Concepción**. Here the ore was smelted into twenty-two carat bars. Concepción was the principal settlement of the province, the Caribbean port of entry for the mines and was populated by thirty souls, which included a governor and other officials.

Drake's force had become rather small for such a dangerous mission, so the majority favoured attacking the lightly armed victuallers. Oxenham in the *Bear*, sailed east towards Tolú, whilst Drake sailed west in the *Minion*, taking up station off the Cabezas, which are near the Holandes Cayos. Drake intercepted a frigate carrying a little gold and a Genoese pilot, who had been at Veragua within the last eight days. Drake eagerly listened to his knowledge of the current state of the harbour and town. This included news that within a few days, a frigate was soon to leave loaded with gold. The Genoese offered to lead Drake to the ship under the cover of darkness through the shallow, tricky channel in exchange for his release. Drake wanted to return to the fort to collect those *cimarrones* who had knowledge of the island but the Genoese emphatically stressed that speed was paramount.

"...the Towne is five leagues within the Harbor,..But when we were to come to the mouth of the Harbor..." [D.R. 314] signal shots were heard. The Genoese thought, because the Spaniards were alert to the continued presence of the English along their coast, Drake's arrival had been spotted. The governor had stationed a sentinel near the harbour bar and sentries up-river to discharge their harquebuses on sighting an approaching sail. Furthermore the wind which had been a helpful easterly, had

changed to westerly and was now contrary for an entry. Once again Drake had to return to *Fort Diego* empty-handed.

Only jungle trails serve this part of Panamá. In Bocas del Toro I had hired a ten metre, open decked, glass fibre boat for a 150 mile excursion in open sea. Its $700 cost was shared by John. This was the first time I had benefited from a significant financial contribution from an accompanying Drake scholar. En route we had conducted field studies on the isolated island of Escudo de Veragua. Surprisingly we had encountered an anchored yacht. The American family had heard of my desire to search for Drake's casket. The River Concepción was thirty-seven miles away. Living off my wits prompted me to ask the skipper for a compass bearing from his large scale chart. Our boatmen followed a course of 116^0. Within 1½ miles east of our landfall we found a picturesque estuary with a sand bar projecting from the east bank, backed by a hamlet of wooden, thatched huts. I told John that I would be delighted if this were Concepción. Emerging from their dwellings a group of curious residents confirmed that we had arrived! They informed us that the old mine up-river was still somewhat productive. The population of 150 provided human life to an environment, which has hardly changed since Drake's night-time probe. Extra pictures were taken with the dark blue filter to simulate darkness. It was easy to visualise the sentinel clutching his harquebus standing on the sand bar surrounded by the sound of waves surrendering themselves to the shallows by toppling into the river mouth as the wind rustled a course through the dense vegetation. Like Drake we sailed eastward but in high spirits, since our mission was a great success!

"Fort Diego"

John Oxenham's venture had yielded a handsome store of victuals aboard a new sturdy Spanish frigate. The next day, 20 March, she was tallowed and armed. Oxenham's prisoners, had stated that two small galleys were being built at Nombre de Dios for trade between that town and the Chagres. Over an Easter Day feast Drake stimulated his company by planning their destruction. The following day, taking the frigate from Tolú and the *Bear*, he sailed for the Cativas.

The Cativas

After threading his way through the network of coral shoals, Drake could have been on <u>Chichime Keys</u> or <u>Porvenir Island</u>. On the second day at midday a sail was discerned approaching the islands from the west. Drake sailed out to meet the ship which was French and commanded by the famous explorer and map-maker, Captain Guillaume Le Têtu. The French, who were in a weakened state and in dire need of water, had heard of the English presence and desired to establish contact. Drake instructed Le Têtu to follow him, *"to the next Port, where he should have both water and victualls."* [D.R. 316] This next anchoring could have been on any island to the east but hopefully and most likely, it was at *Fort Diego*, about nine miles away.

"Fort Diego"

Le Têtu wanted to form an alliance. The French were a force of seventy compared to Drake's thirty-one. Francis warily accepted but stated that what spoils might befall them must be equally divided. Although Drake had fewer men and smaller ships, his bargaining hand was strengthened because he had devised the plan to attack the mule trains, which were now entering Nombre de Dios daily. Francis Drake also had the support of the *cimarrones* and boats small enough for the mission in hand. Drake assembled twenty Frenchmen; fifteen Englishmen and around about forty *cimarrones*.

"Rio Francisco"

They sailed west in the Tolú frigate and two pinnaces bound for the *Rio Francisco*, from where they were to begin their march. A ruttier in Hakluyt, [Vol. VII. 233] correctly sums up the description of the coastline, *"Cabeza de Cativa R. Francisco: It has for markes a certaine land not very high, and within the land certaine high hill lying East and West."* The entrance to the river was too shallow for the frigate, so under the command of Robert Doble it was sent back to the Cabezas and ordered to wait there for the return of the pinnaces. That day of 31 March Drake landed on the west bank of the *River Francisco* and ordered the pinnaces to collect them exactly four days later.

"It is five leagues accounted by Sea, between Rio Francisco and Nombre de Dios, but that way which we marched by land, we found it above seaven leagues." [D.R. 318]

The River Cuango lies at this exact distance from Nombre de Dios. Finding this river was not as routine as I had imagined. Maps from the 17th century show the *River Francisco* to be in several different places. For example it is placed east of the coastline's largest inlet, Port Escribanos, alternatively twenty miles further west, being to the west of Palenque. A map dated 1785 published by Webster [op. cit.] puts the *River Francisco* roughly where the present-day River Cuango is situated but it shows Palenque to be too far to the east. Amid this confusing material the ruttier in Hakluyt, helps to identify, almost beyond doubt, the location of the *River Francisco*.

"And on the West of the river of Francisco thou shalt see certaine cliffes that bee sixe leagues from Nombre de Dios, inclining towards the sea." [op. cit. 233]

By canoe I scrutinised every metre of coastline in the hope of finding this once well-known river. The land is heavily wooded but there are no cliffs. However half a mile west of the River Cuango, is a ledge of low eroded rocks which protrude seaward. As this is a unique, local geographical configuration, I consider that this feature confirms my suspicions that the River Cuango is the *Francisco*. The Cuango is the largest river on this stretch of coast. Sadly, due to the devastating practice of slash and burn, all the estuaries are almost blocked by sand bars. However the depth of the Cuango shows that Drake's pinnaces could have easily penetrated the river.

The Route

Over a day was spent silently marching over low, densely-forested hills, where the torrid heat was tolerated by the thoughts of becoming rich within hours. No doubt numerous snakes were seen, which in my experience were thankfully timid. Initially I viewed Drake's route in general from a light plane that virtually brushed the tree tops. Fortunately most of the jungle remained intact but had been partly cleared for cattle rearing near the road and Nombre de Dios. After more visits to Panamá, with less photography remaining, analysing Drake's route in 1999 became a priority. Previously I had not given the subject much thought because accuracy would be elusive. However I was inspired by John's presence and deductions. Drake required a constant water supply; especially during the hasty escape. Traversing the flattest ground possible for physical ease and speed was another consideration. In 1991 I had purchased maps from Panama University. I was heartened to find a large scale, ordnance survey type map of the Nombre de Dios area. I later learnt that it had been prepared within the last five months by the US Army's National Guard who were building a road from Nombre de Dios to the River Cuango / "Francisco". From this superb map I was inspired to commence the search for: Drake's overnight camp; the site of the ambush and, working away from the known, his route. Hence my fieldwork did not follow the sequence of events in the Drake story.

The National Guard's loose stone road had enhanced a long established trail, that linked the coastal villages. Therefore one can follow much of Drake's most likely route by bus from Cuango village to a mile SE of Nombre de Dios. This map now served to establish Drake's route with great accuracy. From the *River Francisco* the trail follows the coast about 200 metres inland, cutting its way between low hills as it crosses small streams. From the River Zahino, it lies around 700 metres inland. Drake then followed the River Viento Frio to its most westerly point. He then marched 1300 metres west along a valley, where he followed the tributary to the River Fató for 1½ miles. He was now only one mile SE of Nombre de Dios, where he marched nearly 1¼ miles up the River Fató. Here the *cimarrones* knew that they were roughly east of the ambush site and guided Drake almost a mile to a hilltop.

The Overnight Camp

"When we had come within an English mile of the way we stayed all night, refreshing our selves in great stilnes in a most convenient place, where we heard the Carpenters, being many in number, working upon their Ships, as they usually doe by reason of the great heat of the day, Nombre de Dios, & might heare the Moyles comming from Panama, by reason of the advantage of the ground." [ibid]

Regrettably, according to Webster, there are no colonial maps of the Camino nearing Nombre de Dios and this sector had never been paved. Prior to leaving England, I knew that it would be an ordeal to find the hilltop upon which about eighty men slept and where, along the Camino Real, Drake waylaid the mule trains. To complete a nominal attempt I had visions of flying over the area for a general picture. Also a close estimate could be reached by matching the lie of the land with the description of the attack.

Since Drake heard the sounds of the shipwrights at work, I became interested in the two hill tops, which form the ends of a 500 metre long saddle. Its southern end begins at a kilometre from where the Juan-Miguel stream enters the River Nombre de Dios, over 1½ miles south as the crow flies from Nombre de Dios. I hoped that this was near the site of the ambush.

I arrived at Nombre de Dios in a large canoe and was surprised to encounter the American soldiers. They showed an interest in my work. I was introduced to the commanding officer, Lt. Col. Vaughan, from whom I received two night's free accommodation in their jungle encampment. It was like being on the TV filmset for an episode of M.A.S.H. I was given whatever help was available. I desired to be taken through the jungle in search of the encampment. It required the tenacity and compass skills of "pathfinder" trained, Vietnam veteran, forty-five year old Jerry Olson to forge his way up-hill through semi-virgin jungle. As I became tangled in a labyrinth of vines and consequently cut by the coarse vegetation, I was quietly prepared to give up. Jerry did not console my misery, when he said that he did not bother to bring a machete because he would be spending more time hacking than walking! We arrived at the first peak of sixty-eight metres elevation, where at last I enjoyed the luxury of being able to stand erect, as now trees had somewhat receded to grass. I noted that there would not have been sufficient room to sleep around eighty men. Jerry estimated room for twenty. Encouragingly 500 metres to the NE was the other end of the saddle, which was a metre less in

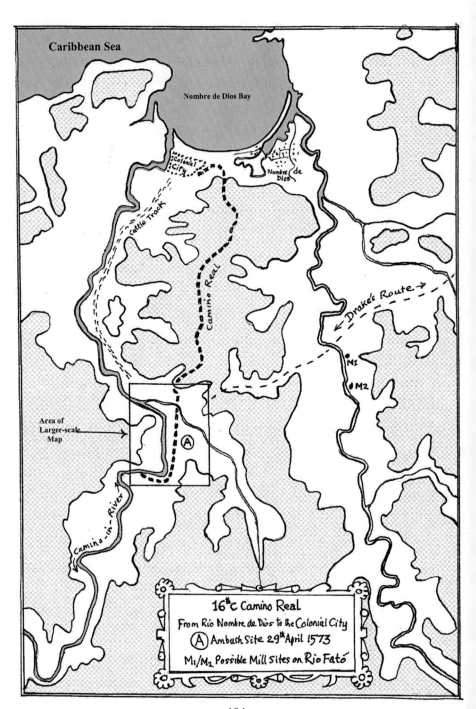

Caribbean Sea

Nombre de Dios Bay

Colonial City

Nombre de Dios

Cattle Track

Camino Real

Drake's Route

M1

M2

Area of Larger-scale Map

Camino-in-River

16ᵗʰ c Camino Real
From Río Nombre de Dios to the Colonial City
Ⓐ Ambush Site 29ᵗʰ April 1573
M₁/M₂ Possible Mill Sites on Río Fató

The Ambush Site

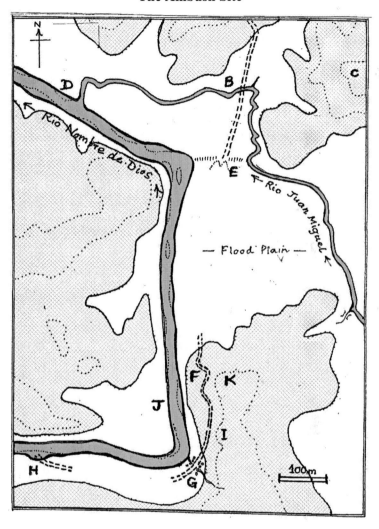

B Camino Real Ford over Rio Juan-Miguel

C Site of Drake's overnight camp 28/29 April

D Junction-Rios Juan-Miguel/Nombre de Dios

E Mule-train cuts on bank of flood-plain

F Camino-Real ascends from flood-plain

G Stone "Bridge" crossing of deep cleft

H Camino Real enters/leaves Rio Nombre de Dios

I High ground from which French probably attacked

J French may have hidden silver in this area

K Defensive position of Spanish rearguard 1596

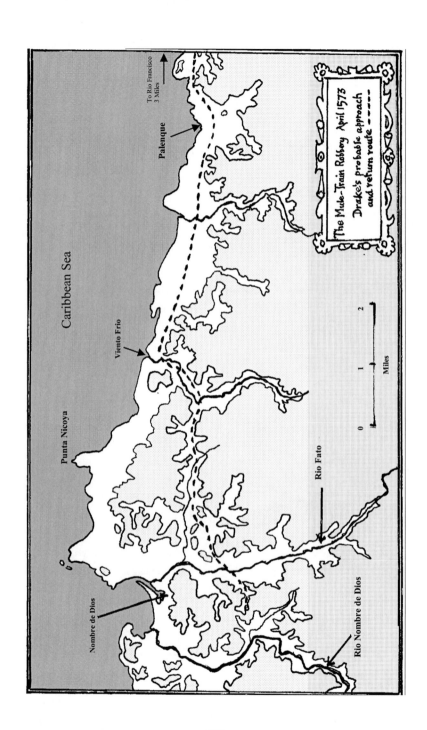

Caribbean Sea

Punta Nicoya

Viento Frio

Palenque

To Rio Francisco
3 Miles

Nombre de Dios

Rio Fato

Rio Nombre de Dios

The Mule-Train Robbery April 1573

Drake's probable approach
and return route -----

0   1   2

Miles

186

height. Before proceeding, I insisted upon compass verification and another one later, when we arrived. Here there was ample room for eighty men to sleep as their dreams of becoming rich were about to be realised. There was a clear view of the coast to the west of Nombre de Dios and the sea could be heard. Therefore in the stillness of the night, it was no exaggeration that the hammers of the shipwrights were heard. Jerry explained that Drake had to sleep on a hilltop because it is the driest part of the landscape, hence the trees give way to shrubs and grass. Also I noticed that it was the only flat ground. This hike was an experience in itself and had shown that this hilltop, at 1,200 metres from the trail, was a contender for Drake's encampment. It fitted the stated distance from the trail; was of a large enough grassed area; and commanded a good view of the approach route from the east. However it may not be far enough from Nombre de Dios. Nevertheless I had closely experienced this part of the story.

"River Campos" = Rivulet Juan - Miguel

The next morning, according to *Drake Revived*, was 1 April, but from the Spanish reports of the ensuing events, it was actually the 29th. The deep sound of the mule bells was heard. The sound, which was synonymous with treasure, must have rung in the minds of the robbers for the remainder of their lives! Drake led his men down to the highway. Soon three pack trains approached: one of fifty and the other two of seventy mules. Each mule carried the standard burden of 300 pounds, making a seizable quantity of nearly thirty tons! The English and French rushed out and grasped the heads of the front and rear mules which caused all the mules to lie down. The Spanish sources admit, that being so close to home had caused the guards to march in a state of disorder. There were fifteen guards escorting each mule train. The forty-five soldiers were bewildered by such a large attack, which the Spanish sources record, happened at the *River Campos* between one and two leagues from their destination. During the short exchange of bullets and arrows, a *cimarron* was killed and Le Têtu mortally wounded in the stomach. The Spaniards nearer the rear of the train fled back to Panamá and the remainder to Nombre de Dios.

Drake had achieved the ultimate by attempting the least expected. The heaviest-laden mules were unloaded first. When Drake attacked Nombre de Dios the previous year, *Drake Revived* states that each silver bar weighed between thirty-five and forty pounds. There was too much to carry, so an estimated fifteen tons of silver was buried, *"...in the boroughs which the great Landcrabs had made in the earth, and partly under old trees which are fallen thereabout, and partly in the sand and gravell of a River, not very deepe of water."* [D.R. 319] A French statement, [cited by Sugden, 73] noted that the French buried some treasure on a tiny island. Since the French were at the rear of the treasure-train, the island was of gravel in the River Nombre de Dios.

At noon, the startled, armour-clad soldiers, all dripping in perspiration arrived at Nombre de Dios to announce the disaster. A force was mustered in the main square. Its number was swelled by residents, who were threatened with death, if they resisted the call of patriotic duty. Drake would have calculated the timing of their arrival. *Drake Revived* states that two hours later, when all the treasure had been buried, which would have been about 1pm, each man loaded himself with all the gold and silver he could carry, to retrace urgently their steps. It can be estimated that, if there were as many as eighty raiders, each man could carry sixty pounds of treasure. It would take five men to carry a mule load. Assuming there were 190 mules, the corsairs could only carry sixteen mule loads bearing 2.14 tons out of thirty. This implies that Drake left behind about 672 bars of silver. For a detailed estimate of weights and modern-day values. [See Appendix 3]

The sounds of horses and foot soldiers were heard. One may wonder if this is a nostalgic Drake using poetic licence to sharpen his story. According to *Drake Revived* the Spaniards did not pursue the robbers into the jungle. Here Le Têtu was left with two devoted followers, in the hope that after a rest, he would be able to travel. After marching two leagues, it was realised that one of the Frenchmen was missing. It was subsequently discovered that he had set off in advance of the party, drunk on wine and overladen. He had become lost and that evening was captured and tortured into revealing the location of most of the buried silver. Again the effects of alcohol were responsible for a loss of treasure. To help appease the king the Spanish reports stated that all the treasure lying on the ground was back in safe custody and that the corsairs were chased two leagues through the jungle until heavy rain curtailed the pursuit. That night, on their return to Nombre de Dios these Spaniards saw on display, the head of Le Têtu and a *cimarron*. Upon arriving at Nombre de Dios they learnt that one of the Frenchmen who had remained with Le Têtu, had been captured, because after Le Têtu had died, he had fled carrying too much treasure. This unfortunate prospector was summarily quartered. Captain Cristóbal Monte reported that the Frenchman was named Jacques Laurens and was seized and handed over to the authorities at Nombre de Dios by Negroes building a dam for a mill on the *Factor's River*. This confirms that the robbery occurred west of the present-day River Fató and that the Frenchman had only travelled one mile.

This was just one of many clues, which made the difficult search for the site of the robbery an irresistible challenge. In 1991 I had concentrated my initial search along the Nombre de Dios, since it was the only river in the area.

Aker has studied the Spanish expeditions of Cermeño and Vizcaino Unamuno, who had contact with California. Whilst ashore these men recorded distances between landmarks in leagues. Aker discovered that the Spaniards were using a land league, which he calculated equalled 1.36 statute miles, which is less than half the distance of a nautical league. Consequently I speculated that the mule train was robbed on the river Nombre de Dios near the sharp bend on its east bank opposite the 34 metre high hill on the west bank. This initial site is over 1½ miles by foot from the town which would have been far enough from Nombre de Dios along what was described as a, *very muddy bad road*. Not much rain is required to make the ground difficult underfoot. In fact, the robbery had occurred just as the rains set in.

By coincidence with *Drake Revived* I had explored the river 418 years to the day and time to when Drake became rich. Therefore the area of dried-up river bed of the Nombre de Dios was somewhat similar, which helped to visualise where and how the silver bars were hidden. Its bed is composed of gravel, sand and pebbles. At the end of the dry season the river covered less than half of its bed. The dry areas of gravel would constitute the *islands*, under which the French buried some of the treasure. The river was generally below knee deep and is in agreement with *not very deepe of water*. However in a few places depths reached two metres. Since the slash and burn had exposed the ground to the baking sun, its dryness no longer attracted as many land crabs hence the holes along the river bank were few. These perennial inhabitants are the blue fiddler crabs.

After my 1991 exploration Dean Edwin Webster wrote stating his belief that the *Campos* was a tributary to the River Nombre de Dios. With so much uncertainty I was glad that I had looked at the River Nombre de Dios, since this would initiate the process of elimination and hopefully lead to a positive identification. Webster argued that the attack would not have occurred on flat ground. The trail would have avoided such low, swampy ground and the quagmire of alluvial mud on the river banks at the end of the wet season. Also the trail would have only followed the river, if its bed was firm. Indeed all the river beds in the area were firm. Webster's opinions were based on the fact that, the existing section of the Camino Real heads south out of Nombre de Dios over hills to the east of the river Nombre de Dios. In fact the first mile of this ancient trail was marked on my map! During Drake's final voyage we learn from Baskerville that the Camino did follow the high ground to the east of the river Nombre de Dios.

"The first League upon the Tope of a mountayn coveryd with wode so narow, that the Breadthe was nott above xxty fote, through which passag was cutte, which being clay with the contynuall going of their reekos and dayly falling of raine is so stary and fowle that every step is above the knee...The next 2

leagues you take up the course of a ryver for the most part up to the girdell..."
[Andrews, The Last Voyage of Drake and Hawkins, 119]

Webster did not accept the notion of a Spanish land league and calculated the site of the ambush in relation to nautical leagues as stated in *Drake Revived*. Therefore the Camino would not have crossed any river for at least two statute miles. This has prompted Webster to speculate that the attack occurred in one of three places. However he admits that his opinions are limited, because he did not have the opportunity to trace this section of the Camino. Nonetheless, compared to my initial study, Webster stated that his sites better suited the distance from Nombre de Dios, as Drake would have needed sufficient time to choose the best of the treasure and bury the remainder before the Spaniards arrived with reinforcements. Webster's first choice was a mile up the aforementioned tributary, where the trail may have left the *Campos* and crossed a ridge towards the River Nombre de Dios. The second and third choices were on either of the two streams before the Pavos and Nombre de Dios unite, being 3.6 miles as the crow flies from the town. As a reconnaissance to part of my planned 1993 expedition, in 1992 I eagerly studied this fork from a plane. I had visions of requiring a guide to reach this area. However most of the jungle has been burnt for cattle farming but trees still lined the rivers and the lie of the land must have remained intact. Steep hills border the rivers and would provide high enough ground, from which the sound of the shipwrights was heard. This river junction would place the robbery up to six miles from Nombre de Dios. This begs the question, could the sound of the shipwrights be heard from around this distance?

During April 1993 John and I eagerly followed the Camino
Real up its tortuous climb out of Nombre de Dios. I used a
compass to avoid passing down three side trails. The red mud
Camino was rutted, wet and slippery in places. I became
optimistic, when the trail continued beyond the distance
depicted on the map. One and a quarter hours and over two
miles into the brisk march the trail descended and, to my
excitement, suddenly overlooked and entered flat ground.
Eighty metres further on the Camino crossed the tributary. This
three metre wide stream called the Juan - Miguel would
qualify as a river in the Drake narratives, because I had visited
other streams that the texts had described as rivers. The
aeroplane survey had confirmed that the tributary follows the
only low and flat terrain in the area. *Campos*, meaning fields,
would have been an appropriate name. Reflecting upon
Webster's opinions, this flat ground was firm during the dry
season and was not much worse underfoot than the higher
ground during the beginning and end of the wet season.
Furthermore this flat and low section of the Camino was very
short. The trail continued straight, south and to the west of the
meandering stream. Halfway down this plain the trail vanished.
This must be due to the "winter" flooding of the River Nombre
de Dios. However, compared with the map, the trail ran for
twice the stated distance. Six years later John and I were to find
remains of the trail leading to the south side of the plain. The
missing 400 metres would be somewhat inconsequential.

To facilitate communication and give less cover to any
retaliatory sniper fire, Drake would have attacked the pack train
along an open, flat and straight section of the trail. John stated
that if there were 190 mules with three metres between each
mule head, then the train would have been at least 600 metres

in length! The Spanish sources reported the number of mules to be over 100.

We presume that the mule train diagonally crossed the plain, or initially it could have followed the lower slopes of the hills on the south edge of the plain before turning north. The Camino then slightly climbed a cut in the NE corner of the plain to travel alongside the Juan - Miguel stream. This would have given Drake 7-800 metres of mule bearing treasure! The plain would have been geographically ideal! Furthermore, due to the mud on either side of the stream and the sudden rise of land eighty metres north of the stream, the mule trains would have been near to a stand-still!

The corsairs were probably standing knee deep in the river, concealed up to their waist by the higher level of the river bank. Long grass would have provided even more cover. Drake was 2½ miles from Nombre de Dios, which agrees with Aker's claim that the Spaniards were using the land league. This distance exactly accords with the Spaniards estimated distance, which varied between one and two leagues. Hence the range of stated distances would agree with the nautical and land league. Webster wrote to me stating that at this distance from Nombre de Dios the town's folk would have heard the shots. Therefore a troop of soldiers would have arrived too soon for Drake's liking. However John stated that the range of hills would have absorbed the sound. Furthermore the firing would have been down wind from the residents.

Assuming that I have at last found the site of the robbery, we can continue to piece together new information. Therefore Drake must have known that it would have taken the Spaniards an hour to reach Nombre de Dios; an hour to muster reinforcements and an hour to return. If the alarm was raised at noon, then the robbery occurred around 11am; meaning that reinforcements had returned at 2pm.

To confirm my findings I visited an isolated house on a hilltop, which overlooked the southern edge of the plain. The occupier kindly guided us to inspect Webster's prime site, over a kilometre further up the tributary. The land was too steep and confined either side of the stream.

We also climbed two hills to the east of the ford in search of the site of the overnight camp. The first was 300 metres east of the Camino. It had a circular top, which was crowned with orange trees. Its size would have accommodated eighty men. Five hundred metres further east there was a long and narrow saddle of similar height. I favoured the former, for reasons of comfort and ability to reach the trail swiftly once the approach of the pack trains had been announced. The camp must have been well *within an English mile of the way* because the corsairs *refreshed themselves in great stilnes,* no doubt to avoid detection from any travellers. From these positions I could hear the mining machinery operating at Nombre de Dios. I felt a sense of spiritual blessing, because this temporary installation was functioning on the site of the market square at such a crucial time! It was a unique occasion, like listening to one's own wedding bells!

John and I had walked about ten miles in ten hours. I now lay in a hammock, gazing across Nombre de Dios bay, replenishing my weary body with sustenance, whilst mulling over the day's achievements. This robbery had propelled Drake towards legendary status and I was convinced that we had been within: sight of the ambush; hearing distance of the harquebus fire; the cries of triumph and only metres away from the remaining bars of silver. Finding a sample would conclusively prove the location of the most audacious robbery in Spanish-American history. This was a compelling reason to return. We could no doubt be accommodated in the hill top farmhouse. With water purifying tablets the stream provided cool water. I had seen two snakes, which posed no problems. However, my head had brushed a branch of a tree overhanging the trail, adjacent to the stream. Thousands of fleas had stung my face and scalp - which all added to the sensation of following Francis Drake!

The following Easter, José, very kindly accommodated us in his farmhouse for two nights. This gave us three days to conduct our search for treasure. We were not allowed to scour the grassy plain, because Don José had made a pact with a man from Panama City, who believed that items of value lay beneath the ground. This gave us heart. We were more than content to restrict our search to the stream. This in itself was no small undertaking. René Gómez of Scubapanamá had borrowed a metal detector for our use. This prevented possible confiscation by the Panamanian customs, if I were to have brought one from England. To keep within the parameters of Law 14 we should have applied for a permit. This would have meant our search being supervised by a government official from the National Museum. Since we were operating in such a secluded area, we wanted to avoid the inherent protracted bureaucracy. The idea was that should we find any silver, we would surrender it to René for safe keeping, whilst we applied for a permit for an official search in the summer. A successful expedition would be assured and would yield the type of world-wide publicity, which my project needs.

John and I probed the 100 metre stretch of the Juan-Miguel stream that flowed beside the Camino. Using John's plastic trowel, which was free with *Gardener's Weekly*, and our bare hands, we removed all the gravel in our thorough effort to reach every target. The next day, José lent us a spade. We had found: a spoon, a torch, batteries, a nail in a wooden post, plenty of barbed wire and corrugated iron. After digging up to our armpits with a constant battle against the current causing our hole to fill in, John hit a solid metal object with the spade. He paused and looked at me with an expression that this could be it! However our hands had only seized the head of a pick axe. This was the closest we had come to a silver bar. I was disappointed. By nature I am an eternal optimist. John consoled me by stating that we had proved that nobody could just come here and find silver with ease. I still felt that we were only metres away from at least one silver bar.

Over 400 years the stream had obviously experienced lateral shift. Hence much or all of the present-day course could be in a totally different place. Along with 400 torrential rainy seasons, the arrival of cattle would have further eroded and moved the banks. Some of the inner meanders were high banks of dry gravel. This meant that a silver bar could be at least a metre deep. If the present-day river banks were over the original bed, an ingot could be at a depth of nearly two metres. Furthermore, the bars could have sunk deeper under their own weight into the mud which lies beneath the gravel. This would have been beyond the range of a standard metal detector.

We also searched a short section half a mile up-stream, which is the spot favoured by Webster. We examined a gravel island on the River Nombre de Dios, roughly where the French had buried silver. Subsequently José guided us to the junction of the Nombre de Dios and Pavos rivers. These water courses were Webster's second and third choices. There was no obvious trail, which either cut across or ran along any river. It took so long to reach this fork that we considered these alternatives to be too far from Nombre de Dios. It would have been impossible to hear the sound of shipwrights at work from a nearby hilltop. Furthermore Drake would have been long gone after the robbery to have heard the approach of Spanish reinforcements. This visit to the junction further consolidated my thinking that I have found the most likely place of the robbery.

The pack train was waylaid between leaving the River Nombre de Dios and climbing into the hills. The length of the train must have occupied all of the plain. Therefore the treasure was buried in two rivers. This indicates that the French had attacked the rear section and like the first ambush near *Venta de Chagres*, Drake had attacked the front half and buried his treasure in the bed of the *Campos*. Pedro knew that this open plain was the only or most suitable place for an ambush along the Camino apart from the site chosen near *Venta de Chagres*.

To prove my conclusions beyond doubt would require finding a silver bar by using more sophisticated detecting equipment. However further research by John Thrower has eliminated any doubts. John's work proves that Drake attacked the mule train on the last land section of the Camino and that this was indeed open country.

Contrary to the imagination of most scholars much of the Camino Real followed firm river beds. In *The Drake Manuscript*, a late 16th century French accounts states, *"It is necessary that the traders coming from Panama to Nombre de Dios pass three fresh water rivers, the water covering half their bodies and they are in danger when the water is high. Men and mules carrying merchandise as well as gold and silver coins are usually submerged in the water."* [266]

This account verifies Baskerville's. Once the Camino had descended the Capirilla Pass, it followed the firm gravel beds of the rivers: Boquerón, Los Pavos and the Nombre de Dios.

Therefore Drake mounted his land attack after the Camino left the River Nombre de Dios to begin its final section on land. The Camino had left the river for two reasons. I discovered the river became too deep in places; since it was nearing the sea. Also the cattle trail beside the river would become too boggy, hence the hills would have been firmer underfoot. Therefore the Camino traversed the open *Campos* flood plain between the River Nombre de Dios before ascending into the hills. In Drake's day this was relatively open country, because at some stage, it was used for cattle grazing.

From Drake's 1595 attack on Nombre de Dios, we read in Andrews [op. cit. 211] a report from Miguel Ruiz Delduayen. *"...the enemy embarked on the beach near the slaughterhouse ...The English advanced by a cattle track to cut the road to Panama and if Captain Quiñones had not warned our men of this they would have been cut off."*

Hence the English were outflanking the route of retreat along the Camino Real by using a cattle track to intercept the Spaniards before they reached the river. Thus the cattle track could only cut the Camino between the hills and the river. This was on the *Campos* plain!

Therefore the landscape would have been very similar to that of today: open grassland, interspersed by a few trees. Furthermore the mud cattle trail still cuts its route between high bushes on the east flood plain of the River Nombre de Dios, until it reaches the *Campos* plain. Admittedly we are backdating 1595 information to support an event in 1573. However the permanent settlers would have required a regular source of fresh meat. From around 1564 this need would have progressively increased with the seasonal arrival of the mule trains and the treasure fleet. Furthermore we know that in 1572, Isla Bastimentos, meaning Island of Provisions, served Nombre de Dios as its market garden. After the Camino was re-routed to Portobelo in 1596, cattle grazing was established to support the new treasure terminus.

John's conclusion amplifies the significance of fieldwork to resolve the limitations of some 16th century accounts.

In 1999 John and I wanted to trace the route of the mules from where the bells were heard to the ambush site. This entailed trying to discover another unknown section of the Camino Real. We searched for what could possibly be considered the remains of a mule cut leaving the River Nombre de Dios. We assumed that the Spaniards would have followed the convenience of the river for as long as possible. Where the river flows east before turning sharply north, we found a beach backed by a mule cut in to the south bank. To consolidate our find, a footpath led just over 300 metres across undulating and descending ground to deliberately placed stones, that infilled to bridge a gully, immediately next to where the River Nombre de Dios turns sharply northwards. There are no other stones in the area. Don José stated that farmers never encounter or use stones for building work. It seems that these stones were deliberately brought into the area long ago. This bridge lies 900 metres SSW of the north edge of the flood plain.

From the bridge the path steeply ascended and led 250 metres north, descending and meandering to the SW corner of the *Campos* plain. Up to this point the land rose on the east side. Hence between here and the stone bridge, was the ideal elevated spot for the French to attack and envelop the rear of the mule train. It was probably here where Le Têtu was shot. The Spanish rearguard was caught between the hills and the river. Their only course of escape was to flee back along the trail into the river towards Panamá. To the north of the bend the French could see the island in the River Nombre de Dios, which was the obvious location to hide their portion of the silver. However the river has laterally shifted towards the east. The remaining bars could now be underneath the west bank.

It is most likely that the Spaniards, who reached Nombre de Dios, did so along the cattle trail. Drake was probably unaware of the riverside route into Nombre de Dios. Drake would have at least blocked the Camino, where it steeply ascends, to prevent the Spaniards from raising the alarm. Here the Camino is only three metres wide. Those who may have blocked the Camino may have become sentries to give advance warning of the approach of Spanish reinforcements.

This fieldwork cemented our conclusions beyond doubt. We had mapped the entire land section of the Camino. Drake had attacked the treasure train on a 1200 metre flat stretch of land; from the riverside cut to where the trail suddenly rises into the hills. This was the only ideal terrain on the Camino, to the north of Drake's first ambush attempt, and of adequate length to accommodate all the mules on flat and open land.

"The Factor's River"

This **River Fató** runs parallel to the *Campos*; a mile to the east. The second time Drake forded this river he was laden with plunder. The corsairs had virtually headed due east and were retracing their route. In January 1996 I wanted to experience these initial moments, when Drake became precariously rich, by following him to the *Factor's River*. From the Quintero family in Nombre de Dios I hired a horse. For my safety and due to my limited riding experience, I was accompanied by the 28 year old son; all for a mere $20. We plodded along the Camino Real, where in places, the horses sank up to their knees in red clay. Although this was the start of the dry season, passage by foot would have been quite impractical. I was pleased to have hired a horse especially, because at first, I thought that I had chosen the lazy option to cover the seven mile journey.

From the ambush site I followed the compass due east. Deviations in direction were caused by too steep gradients, dense vegetation or deep bogs. The corsairs were really tough men! They were fleeing heavily loaded, enduring the tropical, humid, heat and climbing a series of steep hills. Drake then traversed the quarter mile wide flood plain interspersed with bogs. He led his men into the shallow River Fató, which was narrower than the River Nombre de Dios. I had to be within sight of where he entered the river. Drake need not have marched down-river as close as one mile to Nombre de Dios, he could have cut NE between the hills and joined the Fató tributary at a point further east. However he would have still been only 1½ miles from the town. Consequently, it was a daring escape.

In 1999 I rode down-river for the second time to show John Thrower Drake's route. John was very interested to ascertain the possible site of the dam, where the isolated Frenchman had been seized. There were two possible places where the change in land and river bank levels, together with topography, might have made possible, the construction of a mill leat, which was also noted on Drake's last voyage. These are marked on John's Camino Real map as *M1* and *M2*. They are about 300 metres apart and lie within this distance from Drake's route. Hence we can visualise just what a short distance denoted danger.

"Rio Francisco"

"We continued our march all that and the next day towards Rio Francisco,.." [D.R. ibid]

This implies that Drake reached the river the next day, being the 2nd, but the margin reads *April 2, 3*. However both the Spanish sources and *Drake Revived* mention that on the night of the robbery there was a storm, which proves the dates in the margin are at odds with events. This is further supported by some very useful information which I luckily received from the American National Guard. For the seasoned American soldier, wearing better footwear than Drake and his men, it took thirty-six hours, with a night's sleep, to march from Nombre de Dios to the River Cuango, which was also accomplished in the dry season. It is likely that Drake's men were too excited and nervous to sleep, and probably only rested for a few hours. This being the case, Drake although heavily laden, could have covered the twelve miles and arrived at the River Cuango within thirty hours.

To the anxiety of the weary robbers, instead of seeing their own pinnaces, they detected seven Spanish pinnaces. These had been sent from Nombre de Dios to cut off Drake's retreat. It was feared that they had captured Drake's pinnaces, which were sailing from the Cabezas to collect him at the river, as they had been strictly instructed to do this very afternoon. It was easy to imagine that the Spaniards could have captured all of Drake's men, who under torture, would disclose the location of the ships, which would prevent Drake's return to England. The gold would then serve no purpose once marooned in the jungle. Unknown to Drake the night of rain had been driven by a stiff wind, which had prematurely forced the Spaniards to return homeward. Luckily it stopped Drake's pinnaces from even reaching half way. The storm had in fact prevented the Spaniards from finding Drake's pinnaces.

In this desperate situation, the qualities of Drake's leadership emerge to produce a fairy tale story to be etched into the minds of many British school children 400 years later. Drake decided to build a raft, using the trees which were floating down the river as a result of being dislodged by the storm. I wanted to see where such trees toppled into the river.

With the help of the American military, I was taken two miles up the Cuango in a vehicle that miraculously traversed the steep, dense jungle terrain. The river was deep enough for the trees to float to the estuary. This was further confirmed in 1992 when I flew low along the river.

Another reason that the River Cuango is the *Francisco* and not a river nearer to or at Puerto Escribanos is that *Drake Revived* states that they could not reach the pinnaces at Point San Blas by land, *"...because of the Hills, Thickets and Rivers, yet by water."* [D.R. 320] The Cuango is twenty-one miles from Point San Blas. Between Escribanos harbour and the River Cuango there are rivers but not between Escribanos harbour and Point San Blas. The latter two places are only twelve miles apart over flatter land. Hence building a raft would not have been necessary. Upon my return home, I took delivery of the Webster Essays, from which I drew great comfort, when I read that Webster had identified the Cuango as Drake's *Rio Francisco*.

John Smith, two Frenchmen and Pedro the *cimarron* wished to sail with young Francis on this hazardous and critical mission. The objectives were that, if the Spaniards had captured Drake's men, it might still be possible to reach the ships before his men confessed all to the Spaniards or, simply to find his pinnaces. The raft bore a biscuit sack for a sail and a small tree served as a rudder.

Point San Blas

Helped by the west wind and current, the raft made rapid progress, being much faster than the stated estimated three leagues in six hours. They battled against the surges of water, which washed their armpits. In the evening darkness Francis spotted his pinnaces, which did not notice the little raft. Due to the contrary wind, the pinnaces *"...were forced to run into cover behind the point, to take succour for that night; which our Captaine seeing, and gathering, because they came not forth againe, that they would Anchor there, put his raft a shore, and ran by land a-bout the point, where he found them,.."* [D.R. 321] Once aboard, Francis casually dispelled the notion of another disaster by taking out from his shirt a quoit of gold and thanking God for the outcome of the voyage.

Prior to coming to Panamá Mr Aker had stated that the point around which Drake ran and hailed to be taken aboard was undoubtedly Point San Blas. To my disappointment there are only three beaches of twenty metres in length. Otherwise the coast is chiefly of mangroves backed by rocky, jungle-clad hills. Correct interpretation of the geography would suggest that Drake landed on a small beach within a mile of the point, ran a mile across, or around the 200 feet high peninsula and signalled to his pinnaces, which could have harboured in the inlet 1½ miles west of the point. In order to create moody, nocturnal pictures, I arrived on the point's south side half an hour before sunset on a compass bearing from the Cartí river. The canoe put me ashore on a tiny beach just east of the bay's entrance. The dark blue photographic filter made the sinking sun look like the moon. Views of where Drake's ships were anchored were taken from the hills under great personal discomfort. Whilst my sweaty, soil-coated hands were experimenting with the lens filters, I was being pinched all over by swarms of biting fleas. I wondered if during Drake's overland run he had been attacked by these night-time pests. In order to follow the story which facilitates slide filing, I then pursued Drake's route as he skirted the point's east tip, upon which is the only other beach. The camera then followed Drake westward en route to collect his men.

"Rio Francisco" to "Fort Diego"

That night in the early hours of 4 April Drake had sailed and rowed back to the *River Francisco* to embark his jubilant, hero-worshipping men. The Spanish sources claim that in boats they searched the entire length of the *River Francisco*. This would have been before Drake had arrived, after he had left, or maybe when Drake was embarking his men.

Alvaro Flores intriguingly reported that a Negro king had captured an Englishman who stated that Drake did not enter the *Francisco*, but the neighbouring Sardinilla inlet and had concealed his launches under the branches of trees. This was not true, since Drake had sent his craft away for four days. *Drake Revived* makes no mention of a lost Englishman but of a Frenchman. However, it would seem that the Spanish reports had been somewhat fabricated to disguise their inept response to capture the perpetrators of the biggest and most daring robbery ever of American-Spanish treasure.

By dawn the English had reached the frigate anchored near Porvenir Island. At *Fort Diego* Drake divided the weight of the gold and silver between the two forces. The French sailed homeward with their estimated £20,000. The next two weeks were spent preparing the ships for the voyage home. The stores from Drake's original ship were transferred to the Tolú frigate and the former vessel given to the Spanish prisoners.

The Cabezas

Several days were spent riding among these reefs capped by sandy islands. Meanwhile Drake made a secret arrangement that twelve Englishmen and sixteen *cimarrones* were to return to the scene of the ambush with the objectives of finding the buried silver and perhaps Captain Le Têtu.

The hired plane enabled an encapsulating prospect to be recorded of these most seaward of the San Blas Islands. Beautiful tranquil detail was added by a visit in a high speed boat from Porvenir.

"Rio Francisco"

This expedition was led by John Oxenham and Thomas Sherwell because Drake's men thought it best if their captain did not go. Therefore Drake rowed the party to the river and set them ashore. Upon landing they were approached by one of the two Frenchmen who had remained behind to comfort his captain. He fell at Drake's knees thanking him for delivering him from certain death. The Frenchman had only escaped by jettisoning his share of the treasure and running for his life. He estimated that near two thousand Spaniards and Negroes had been ordered to dig for the lost silver. When Drake's men arrived, they noticed that the earth had been dug in every likely place for a mile radius. Nonetheless three days after their departure, Oxenham returned bearing thirteen bars of silver and a few quoits of gold. This was the last recorded fruitful search, which suggests that patient use of a metal detector could yield artifacts pertaining to a most unforgettable day in Drake's life and in English history.

"Rio Grande" de la Magdalena, Colombia

Drake resolved to visit the *Rio Grande* to capture victuals for the homeward voyage. En route, Drake chanced upon the French ship. They finally parted near the **San Bernados Islands**. Drake defiantly exposed himself in full view of the Spanish fleet that was anchored in Cartagena harbour. He flew the flag of St. George and all his streamers to flaunt the Spaniards, as if publicly conveying a signal of victory for his cause. Two leagues before the river, *"...being all low land, and darke night,.."* [D.R. 324] Drake hoisted a small sail as not to overshoot the estuary, whilst waiting for the morning. However he was able to capture an unsuspecting frigate loaded with a variety of provisions. Some of the Spaniards fled ashore but the remainder had nothing to fear. *"The next morning, as soone as we set those Spaniards a shore on the maine, we set our course for the Cabezas..."* [ibid] where five days later they arrived.

From the hired boat out of Flores I had photographed the lagoon, backed by low, undulating land. Drake may have landed the men, where he had previously received cattle from the Indians.

The Cabezas, Panamá

This anchorage was probably at *Fort Diego*, where a week was spent careening, tallowing and trimming the rigging of the two frigates on the waveless beach. The pinnaces were burnt so that the *cimarrones* could have the ironwork. Drake bestowed gifts of linen and other domestic commodities upon Pedro and his followers. They bade their final farewells, expressed their mutual thanks and admiration for each other's cause. Drake set sail carrying Diego, who was to accompany him on his greatest voyage. In response to those who criticise Drake for being involved in the slave trade, it must be noted that Drake was the first Englishman to work with and respect Negroes as equals. Drake knew that the Negroes had been the key to his success. Periodically throughout his life Drake was to exhibit a respect and compassion for peoples of all cultures; and even towards his enemies. Compared to: Colombus, Pizarro, Hawkins and Grenville, Drake's moral behaviour was ahead of his time.

Cape San Antonio, Cuba

*"...we set sayle towards Cape Saint Anthony, by which we past
with a large wind. But presently, being to stand for th'havana,
we were faine to ply to the windward some three or foure
dayes;.." A small bark carrying over 200 hides was taken.
After being unloaded, the vessel was released. " And so
returning to Cape S. Anthony and landing there, we refreshed
our selves, and besides great store of Turtles egges, found by
day in the* [sand?] *we tooke 200. and 50. Turtles by night. We
powdred and dryed some of them, which did us good service."*
[D.R. 325]

Drake landed within site of the present-day lighthouse, during
the nesting season, between May and October. Unfortunately I
was one month too early to witness the egg laying. Living in
England had not enabled me to visualise Drake's contact with
the turtle. Luckily I was to enter free of charge the world's only
turtle farm on Grand Cayman Island. Here the educational
experience provided the pictorial stimulus.

The turtle can lay 100 eggs at once and commonly up to one
thousand per season. This entails between three and six nests a
season. The eggs are laid at night. They look like table tennis
balls and weigh one ounce each. The nest site is above high
water mark on a secluded beach. The flippers are used to dig a
hole two or three feet deep. The sun incubates the nest for two
months, when the newly born turtles take two to three days to
reach the surface.

The egg laying turtles were snatched along the cape's two mile long yellow sand beach. It would seem that to collect 500 eggs only between two and five nests were found.

From here Drake sailed home. En route he had intended to touch at Newfoundland for water but heavy rain collected in the sails, cancelled this necessity. Since I always plan the next Drake expedition before arriving home from the present journey, it is easy to assume that Drake's ideas to reach the Pacific were fermenting, whilst looking at the empty sky and horizon during the uneventful crossing.

Plymouth

About four weeks after leaving Cape San Antonio, Drake with only thirty men arrived home to a quaint welcoming by a jubilant and curious congregation on Sunday 9 August.

"...the newes of our Captaines returne brought unto his, did so speedily passe over all the Church, and surpasse their minds with desire and delight to see him, that very few or none remained with the Preacher, all hastning to see the evidence of Gods love and blessing towards our Gracious Queene and Countrey, by the fruite of our Captaines labour and successe."
[D.R. 326]

This was St Andrew's Church which stands about a quarter of a mile from the inner harbour. This large church is well preserved. To simulate the story I used a tripod to photograph a Sunday morning congregation from the back of the nave.

Several months were spent in Plymouth settling the accounts of the voyage. Two of the Spanish ships were sold to Sir Arthur Champernowne and John Hawkins and Drake kept the third. Drake invested in property and built ships which he hired out. On 12 February 1574 Drake was appointed executor of John's will. Time was also spent managing the affairs of deceased brother Joseph.

Chapter Six

IRELAND

Introduction

Drake's return to Plymouth laden with treasure; most of which
he had lifted from the trans-Panamanian isthmus mule trains,
was a testimony to his personal war with Spain. The Spanish
accounts still do not refer to Drake by name. However, as
Drake was becoming a West Country heroic legend, it would
only be a matter of time, before Spanish diplomats, would learn
who was responsible for this unprecedented spate of pillaging.
Drake's return was an embarrassment to the queen's policy of
conciliation with Philip. Trade with Spain had improved.
Therefore it was politically expedient if Drake and the treasure
were to disappear officially. Consequently, we lose sight of
Drake's movements for nearly two years. The sources are
mainly from the contemporary biographers.

Ireland was in a state of savage turmoil. The Irish Catholics,
aided by the Catholic Scots, were violently resisting the brutal
English Protestant, colonial campaign. This was because
Protestant England considered Catholic Ireland as a potential
base, from which to invade England's vulnerable western flank.

Ulster proved to be the most rebellious part of Ireland. Under
Elizabeth's parsimonious government, Ireland was being
conquered in the spirit of private enterprise. The queen was
earmarking land to the commanders in advance of it being
subdued. The Crown granted the Earl of Essex the lands from
Belfast to Rathlin Island. His expedition set out from Liverpool

in 1573. Initially, the Irish chiefs successfully resisted being governed by the Protestant English. They were supported by the Scots, who used Rathlin Island as a staging post. Their chief, Sorley Boy MacDonell, considered the island safe enough to be used as a sanctuary for the clan's wives and children. The island's stronghold was Bruce's Castle: named after Robert the Bruce, who allegedly took refuge here.

Plymouth

The operation to capture the storm-swept, rocky island, evolved on 8 October 1574. Essex required ships and men. He turned to the West Country ports. To assemble and mobilise his force he communicated with the Vice-Admiral of Devon, Sir Arthur Champernowne. Now owner of one of Drake's captured Spanish frigates, Champernowne obviously knew that marine merchant, Caribbean guerrilla fighter and privateer, Francis Drake, was the most suitably qualified logistician. Furthermore Drake's experience of operating in shallow seas and rivers would be vital to rid the Irish coast of the Scottish galleys. For the first time Essex mentions Drake in his communication with the Privy Council. Furthermore Essex was father-in-law to Drake's godfather, the Earl of Bedford. Drake later stated that he was recommended to Essex by John Hawkins. This further suggests that Hawkins bore no ill feeling over their separation at San Juan de Ulua.

Essex assembled about six vessels and Drake had offered his services. Essex employed Drake for a monthly wage of 42/- from 1 May until the end of September 1575. From his private Caribbean venture Drake was already rich and did not primarily enlist for financial gain. However Drake was now part of a political and military government campaign, through which the accumulation of influence with the leading figures would gain entry into the circles of power that revolved around the queen's court. This was the route Drake needed to gain government backing for his Pacific adventure.

The force presumably cleared Plymouth. Drake was commanding the *Falcon,* which was described as a naval bark or frigate. One of its twenty-five crew was the ten year old son of Drake's Uncle Robert. Cousin John served as Drake's page boy.

Dublin

This augmentative squadron arrived in Dublin on 8 May 1575.

Carrickfergus

Essex originally intended to rid the Scottish galleys from the sea and to isolate the garrison on the Rathlin Island. He now decided to storm the island and fortify it as an English stronghold. Hence the squadron sailed north to Carrickfergus. On 18 July 1575, a force under John Norris arrived with orders from Essex to be embarked for Rathlin Island. The fleet cleared the harbour on 20 July.

Drake would still recognise Carrickfergus. The quaint and picturesque circular harbour with its cobbled wharf is dominated by a superbly preserved Norman castle.

Church Bay, Rathlin Island

Two days later the force of 300 soldiers and eighty horsemen arrived. The island is L-shaped, one mile wide, seven miles long and located six miles NE of Ballycastle, being three miles from the mainland.

Due to high winds in October 1984, I could not visit the island until my next opportunity in the following April. The island was reached by a scheduled service in an open boat. The island's main anchorage is the little harbour inside the mile long Church Bay on the south shore, which is exposed to the prevailing SW winds. The population of the island was 100 and has hardly grown since Drake's arrival. Its remoteness and bleakness, seem to have deterred development which has left it unspoiled. Its bird life remains as prolific.

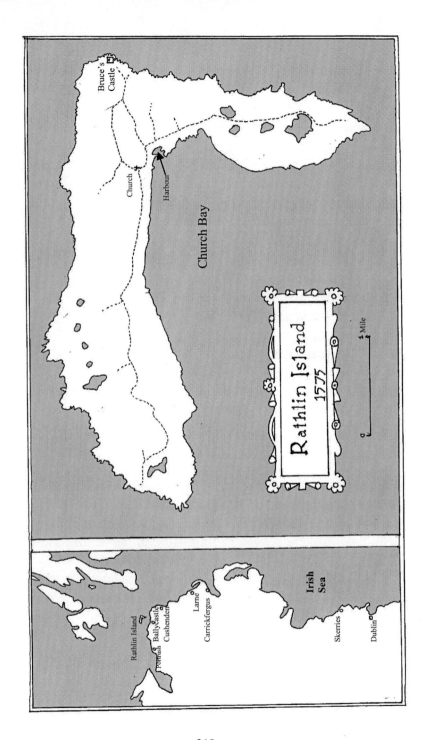

Bruce's
Castle

Church

Harbour

Church Bay

Rathlin Island
1575

¼ Mile

Rathlin Island

Ballycastle
Cushenden
Portrush

Larne

Carrickfergus

Irish
Sea

Skerries

Dublin

218

Church Bay and a pebble-strewn cove 400 metres south, in sight and thus within firing range of the castle, are the only two landing beaches upon the island. Therefore the two heavy siege guns were landed out of sight at Church Bay.

Reaching the castle involved a mile trek over undulating heath land to the NE coast. Bruce's Castle nestles strategically upon a 100 metre high circular cliff and is approached by passing along a twenty metre long by three metre wide rock saddle. Its base is barely about ninety square metres. Only the lower castle walls remain with a window. The natural environment easily enables the visitor to visualise what happened.

It took three days to knock an entry breach into the wall. On the afternoon of 25 July the English were repulsed as they tried to enter the breach. Before dawn the following morning, the besieged asked for terms of surrender, which Drake - as his past and later campaigns demonstrated, would have accepted. The defeated wanted safe passage back to Scotland, the coastline of which they could see thirteen miles away. However the history of battles in Ireland sadly portrayed a lack of honour and mercy by the victors.

Norris knew that the defendants would be vanquished in battle or starved into submission. Furthermore there was no well and water had to be brought from the mainland. The castle had offered stiff and costly resistance to the English and the survival of Scottish souls would rest upon the mood of the captors.

The garrison surrendered and the 200 souls were slain, along with the 300 petrified wretches hiding in the island's cliff face caves. During the massacre Drake is believed to have helped burn eleven Scottish galleys, which arrived to support the stronghold. Drake then oversaw the embarkation of some of the island's livestock and corn, reputedly sufficient to feed 200 men for a year. Due to the steep climb, only light supplies could have been landed at the pebble-strewn cove to re-stock the fort.

Drake was now sailing between the island and Carrickfergus conveying timber, bricks and lime for the fortification of the castle. With a garrison of eighty soldiers, Norris intended to hold the castle for Essex. The latter subsequently agreed. Drake was also engaged in patrolling the island to ensure that the supply lines were free from the retaliatory Scots. Drake was also providing an escort for the boats supplying the island.

Skerries

A document cited by Sugden shows that Drake transported the new Lord Deputy, Sir Henry Sidney. Since <u>Bristol</u> and <u>Liverpool</u> were the ports used to reinforce the campaign, Drake may well have visited them. Sidney was landed at Skerries, fourteen miles north of Dublin on the morning of 7 September.

My two visits to Ireland during unsettled weather, concluded my study of Drake's movements. However, when Sugden consequently discovered the Sidney document, I knew that I would have to make a third visit to Ireland. The isolation of the port, surrounded by an untouched green landscape, meant that Drake could still recognise the port.

Sidney dismantled the garrison on Rathlin and discharged the frigates.

Contemporary historian John Stow, implied that Drake was engaged in other military events. Sugden perceives that this is exaggerated. *"...immediately on his* [Drake's] *return* [from Panamá] *he furnished at his own expense, three frigates with men and munitions, and served voluntarily in Ireland under Walter Earl of Essex, where he did excellent service both by sea and land at the winning of divers strong forts."* [Benson, 97]

It must be remembered, that Drake sold two ships but may have still owned three more. No forts are mentioned by name. My visits to Ireland embraced the *divers strong forts* along the Antrim coast, some of which at least Drake saw in combat or in passing. They are detailed in a south to north-westerly order. It is emphasised that, apart from the Rathlin campaign and Skerries, there is no evidence to reveal Drake's exact whereabouts. What follows is supposition based upon Stow's account.

Olderfleet Castle, Larne

All that remains is a 16th century tower house which is situated adjacent to the modern port.

Portaferry Castle, Cushendunn

Only meagre remnants of a blockhouse remain. The foundations are perched on an islet some thirty metres across, being about forty metres from the shore.

Kinbane Castle, Ballycastle

Its fairly extensive and well preserved ruins of a tower and walls are superimposed on a protruding finger-like rock. It is surrounded by sea at high water.

Dunseverick Castle

This is situated at the east end of Giant's Causeway and sits on a cliff corner. This military relic, only consists of two ruined walls and a tower.

Dunluce Castle, Portrush

The large and well conserved remains precariously occupy the cliff top. Long ago, its kitchen fell into the sea.

Drake's Pool

Sir Julian Corbett wrote about Drake's Pool. A few miles up the Owenboy river towards Cork in southern Ireland, is a wide meander flanked by woodland called Drake's Pool. It is not known for how long this name has been in existence. According to Corbett, this river in Tudor times was a notable haunt for filibusters. Tradition states that, Drake used to hide here and pounce upon Spanish ships. The credibility of this legend is diluted by the on-site Cork Council plaque which reads,

It is to this secluded basin, that Sir Francis Drake is reputed to have led a small squadron of five ships, which had been chased into Cork Harbour by a Spanish fleet of superior force in 1589.

The Spaniards being unacquainted with the harbour, sailed around the shores and finally abandoned the chase, leaving the English fleet safely moored here in the shelter of Curabinny.

From copious contemporary sources, we know that in 1589 - fourteen years after he had returned from Ireland, Drake was leading a retaliatory armada of around 150 ships along the Iberian peninsula.

Plymouth

In the autumn of 1575, Essex failed to subdue the Catholics and Drake returned to Plymouth. Essex returned to Ireland in 1576 and amid broken dreams, died of dysentery. Drake had lost his patron but had spoken to Essex and his aide, Thomas Doughty, whom he met in Ireland, about his desire to prosecute his private and far more profitable war with Spain, by sailing in to the Pacific. Doughty was a soldier and became secretary to the queen's rising favourite courtier, Captain of the Guard, Christopher Hatton. In 1576, Doughty was able to expedite Drake's plan by giving him access to the powerful personalities of Elizabeth's government. For a year Drake oscillated between his Plymouth town house and the London area.

Political events were to unfold that enabled Drake to complete one of the most famous voyages in English history: that of circumnavigating the world.

DEFINITIVE BIBLIOGRAPHY OF PRINCIPAL PRIMARY SOURCES
(in order of life and voyages)

Spanish Documents Concerning English Voyages to the Caribbean 1527-1568
Ed. by I. Wright
Hakluyt / Kraus Reprint, Liechtenstein, 1967

Documents Concerning English Voyages to the Spanish Main 1569-1580
Ed. by I. Wright
Hakluyt / Kraus Reprint, Liechtenstein, 1967

The Plymouth Black Book, The Widney Papers and *The Plymouth Municipal Records - Collected Papers*
West Devon Record Office, Plymouth.

The Last Voyage of Drake & Hawkins
Ed. by K. R. Andrews
Hakluyt Society / Cambridge University Press, 1972

VOYAGES MISCELLANEOUSLY PRESENTED

The Principal Navigations, Voyages, Traffiques & Discoveries of the English Nation
R. Hakluyt,
J. M. Dent & Sons, 1927, London, (8 vols.)

Vol. 6 Narratives by Job Hortop and Miles Philips

Vol. 7 Account by John Hawkins of his 1567-8 voyage

SELECT BIBLIOGRAPHY OF SECONDARY SOURCES

(* contains primary sources)

Andrews, K. R   *Drake's Voyages - a re-assessment of their place in Elizabethan Maritime Expansion*
Weidenfeld & Nicolson, London, 1967

Barrow, J.   *The Life & Exploits of Sir Francis Drake**

John Murray, London, 1861

Benson, E. F   *Sir Francis Drake*
John Lane The Bodley Head, London, 1927

Bradford, E   *Drake*
Hodder & Stoughton, London, 1965

Coote, S   *Drake*
Simon & Schuster, London, 2003

Corbett, J   *Sir Francis Drake*
MacMillan, London, 1936

Corbett, J   *Drake & The Tudor Navy* (2 vols.)
Longman, London, 1899

Cummins, J   *Francis Drake*
Weidenfeld & Nicolson, London, 1995

Gosse, P   *Sir John Hawkins*
                  John Lane The Bodley Head, London,
                  1930

Hampden, J   *Francis Drake Privateer* *
                  Eyre Methuen, London, 1972

Harris, H. J   *Drake of Tavistock*
                  Devon Books, Exeter, 1988

Kelsey, H.   *Sir Francis Drake The Queen's Pirate*
                  Yale University Press, London, 1998

Kraus, H. P   *Sir Francis Drake - A Pictorial*
                  Biography *
                  N. Israel, Amsterdam, 1970

Lewis, M   *The Hawkins Dynasty*
                  George Allen & Unwin, London, 1969

Mason, A. E. W   *The Life of Francis Drake*
                  Hodder & Stoughton, London, 1941

Sugden, J   *Sir Francis Drake*
                  Barrie & Jenkins, London, 1990

Thomson, G. M   *Sir Francis Drake*
                  Secker & Warburg, London, 1972

Thrower, J   *The Lost Treasure of Sir Francis Drake*
                  A Thrower Publication, Powerstock, 1996

Unwin, R   *The Defeat of John Hawkins*
                    George Allen & Unwin, London, 1962

Whitfield, P   *Sir Francis Drake*
                    British library, London, 2004

Williamson, J. A   *Sir John Hawkins: The Time and The
                    Man* *
                    Clarendon Press, Oxford, 1927

Williamson, J. A   *Hawkins of Plymouth*
                    Adam & Charles Black, London, 1949

OTHER SECONDARY SOURCES

Aker, R   *The Aker Letters to Michael Turner*
                    Palo Alto, California, USA, unpublished,
                    1983-98

Anderson, C. L. G   *Old Panama & Castillo del Oro*
                    North River Press, New York, 1938

Barber, J   *Sir Francis Drake's Investment in
                    Plymouth Property*
                    in, Transactions of the Devonshire
                    Association, cxiii, 1981

Gill, C   *Plymouth A New History, Vol. 1*
                    David & Charles, Newton Abbot, 1979

Humble, R   **A 16th Century Galleon**
                   Simon & Schuster, Hemel Hempstead,
                   1993

Jackson, S   **The Jackson Letters to Michael Turner**
                   Telford, England, unpublished, 1993-96

Masefield, J   *On The Spanish Main*
                   Conway Maritime Press, London, 1906

Thrower, J   *The Thrower Letters to Michael Turner*
                   Powerstock, Dorset, England,
                   unpublished, 1992-98

[Author unknown]   *The Drake Manuscript* *
                   Andre Deutsch, London, 1996

[Author unknown]   *Tourist Brochure*, published by, City
                   Council of Rochester upon Medway
                   Leisure Services Department. (not dated)

[Author unknown]   Tourist Brochure, *A Day Out on the
                   Historic Barbican* published by the
                   Barbican Traders' Guild. (not dated)

The 11 volumes of Sailing Directions are published by,
The Hydrographic Department, Ministry of Defence
Taunton, Somerset, England. They also kindly supplied
photocopies of charts.

APPENDIX I

The Expeditions

It has taken 8,000 slides to document photographically all of Drake's life. From the onset all slides were catalogued, accompanied by detailed descriptions from the contemporary narratives. This was in case I needed the information for a book. My first efforts to write this book occurred during a free lesson in school. In an hour I compiled a 1,500 word report about the then, recent and eventful 1986 summer expedition. Other expedition reports were compiled. Typists would assist in their presentation. Soon variations in detail appeared and additions were required. Such manipulation of text was beyond the scope of willing but busy typists. In 1988 I invested in a word processor and was able to compose the book with a high degree of presentation and uniformity. Since the manuscripts were built around each expedition, they included an introduction, sometimes a summary and always a conclusion. In the summer of 1997 these expedition reports were "spilled" into the chronological format of a biography. Consequently to remind myself and explain to the reader how these expeditions chronologically arose these journey outlines have been thankfully, retained in the appendices.

DRAKE IN ENGLAND: ENGLAND AND IRELAND

[1980 - to date]

Introduction

Being from Burnham-on-Sea, Somerset, I am lucky to live within a 1½ hour drive from Plymouth. However during the earliest years, when I had just graduated as a teacher, I reached some of the West Country Drake sites by hitch-hiking, carrying a well beaten, old brown suitcase, which contained an elite camera system and items to sustain me in bed and breakfast for a couple of days. Soon my new friend, Khaldia Boukenine, drove me around Drake's England and twice around Ireland. Later I had a very obliging friend to drive me in her car. After buying my first car in 1988, I enjoyed great independence in reaching the more isolated sites. In later years I enjoyed driving around southern England to visit other Drake places. Boat hire was necessary to document the battle with the Spanish Armada. Unlike travelling in primitive developing countries, the spirit of adventure was, in comparison, minimal. The further away from home I was in Drake's wake or footsteps the greater the sensation. On the other hand rural southern England is full of beautiful Drake places; all of which on sunny days provided stunning photography.

WEST AFRICA

[Summer 1989 & February 1997]

Introduction

I visited all of the Drake anchorages from the latitude of Cape Verde northwards to Cádiz, Spain. Once again I set out from Cape Verde but this time travelling south to Liberia. From here I intended to fly home via Morocco to study two capes, which were previously omitted, due to insufficient time.

Twelve locations was the objective: nine of which feature on the Hawkins and Drake 1567-8 slaving voyage and the remainder being Drake's world voyage.

I had misgivings about executing this journey during the long summer school holidays, because it was West Africa's rainy season and the wettest region on Earth. This makes some mud roads impassable and life extremely uncomfortable with the oppressive humidity, accompanying temperatures of over 30 ^{0}. However, six weeks would provide enough time to wait for bright skies, in trying to emulate the brightness when the Hawkins voyage was here in the dry season. I could even settle for a bright overcast, because Hawkins would not have only experienced blue sky but, a blue-white sky with hazy views, that limited the visibility. This is caused by the North East Trade Winds blowing the sand-laden Harmatten wind from the Sahara Desert. Furthermore Drake was in Liberia and returned to Sierra Leone in wet July. Blue sky with maximum visibility can only be guaranteed at the end of November and in April. The latter month is then too hot and Drake was not here during this photogenic period. Over seven years later I supplemented the slaving voyage slides by returning to all the places south of Cape Roxo at the same time of year as Drake and Hawkins.

Some of the photography was of river estuaries, at least four miles wide, bordered by low and featureless mangrove coastlines, which in the best of weather would only produce repetitive empty pictures. There would nearly always be bright tropical light, in which to record the intriguing primitive and picturesque culture of Black West Africa, which Hawkins witnessed as he mercilessly rounded-up the river bank dwellers for slavery.

Despite my apprehensions, I left England somewhat optimistic, knowing also that the reward could be a final coverage of West Africa.

Conclusion

Hitherto the 1989 expedition was the least enjoyable. Time was frequently spent disorientated in the jungle of African bureaucracy. Bribes, permits, obstinate racist boatmen and inconvenient currency regulations had to be surmounted. This was coupled with being monetarily pestered by the uneducated. Many hours were consumed waiting in hot, sticky, crowded and dirty conditions for equally descriptive transport to traverse hundreds of miles of wet, rutted mud tracks through bland landscape. There were no discoveries but clarifications at the Los Islands and Sierra Leone.

However I had practically seen or visited every Drake anchorage in West Africa. Furthermore, several sights seen in passing were included, which transcended the project's criterion of reaching just the anchorages. Returning home with another pictorial chapter written made it all worthwhile. The 1997 expedition was far more enjoyable.

COLOMBIA, CURAÇAO & VENEZUELA

[Summers 1981, 1984, Winters 1995-6, 1991-2, 8]

Introduction

This region had to be visited seven times before all Drake's anchorages were reached. The Colombian coast was included on my first Drake journey in August 1981, when as always I took photographs. Commercial intentions soon converted me to slides. This necessitated a return visit in summer 1984. However I arrived home eleven days early with only one third of the pictures, due to being wounded and robbed by two blacks with switchblades. After eighteen months of anxiety, I returned for a fruitful two week Christmas study.

I now considered that the coasts of Colombia, Venezuela and Curaçao were complete. Nearly three years later, my illusions were shattered. Although studies of Drake's life were virtually finished, I encountered Job Hortop's account of the Hawkins slaving voyage and Richard Hakluyt's narration of Drake's last expedition. These revealed additional anchorages and very detailed coastal descriptions.

Consequently plans for a West Indies venture were postponed and the studious preparations diverted. I had to return to the dangers of the cocaine and contraband trafficking region of the Guajira, Colombia, where even ordinary people frequently carried side-arms. Despite these journeys, minute detail was still missing. However satisfaction was achieved by January 1991 when 99% of the material from this most intense Drake region had apparently been assembled. Proof-reading in 1998 revealed that I needed more pictures from the sea. Hence I returned to Borburata in Venezuela; Santa Marta and the River Grande de la Magdalena in Colombia. Having recently obtained a GPS, I was encouraged to reach the theoretical distances along this river.

Project methodology has to mature over the years to realise the pinnacle of thoroughness. A return visit encourages the use of more camera angles. For example now that I am no longer a student school teacher, I can bear the cost of boat and plane hire to secure a "Drake's eye view." Covering the same ground enables previous slide exposures to be improved upon and the expansion of a duplicate set. This guards against loss or damage, which would mean yet another return expedition. Each journey adds to the personal adventures in realising the project's objectives.

The region was known in Drake's time as Tierra Firme or romantically by the English as the Spanish Main. Drake's bows ploughed their furrows through the Caribbean on seven voyages between 1566 and 1596. Each anchorage is described chronologically and not in order of my visits.

The 1981 journey included taking photographs in Perú and Ecuador. These would have to be replaced by slides.

Conclusion

For two reasons the repetitive field work became expensive.
Firstly I could not procure the written material at the same pace
as each expedition launch. Seven out of twelve Drake voyages
were destined for the Caribbean, hence the wealth of material
to sift and photograph reached enormous proportions. Secondly
the duration of the holidays was never sufficient. The positive
result of the repeated visits meant the project incorporated the
pinnacle of thoroughness.

PANAMÁ

[Easters 1991, 92, 93 & 94, January 1996, with reference to
August 1981 & 1983, December 1998 & April 1999]

Introduction

Francis Drake spent more time and visited more places in
Panamá than any other foreign country. Upon the project's
inception I realised that after Cape Horn and Indonesia,
Panamá would be the next most inaccessible region, due to the
many offshore islands and the absence of roads on the
mainland. In the rainy season of 1981 I visited many of the
Drake sites which were served by road. I returned exactly two
years later to replace the photographs with slides. It was whilst
toiling under the intense humidity that I realised how hardy and
determined our treasure-hungry ancestors were. The hardships
endured by Elizabeth's robust subjects were seldom conveyed
in the contemporary accounts. I left Panamá knowing that to
complete the photography I would require logistical support,

which may be forthcoming towards the end of the project when my reputation and credentials may attract help.

By 1991 I was still very much on my own but had accumulated experience, knowledge and confidence gained from reaching past, progressively isolated locations. This, coupled with greater financial resources, encouraged me to tackle most of the remaining locations, which could be reached in two week visits. I had learnt of the light aircraft flights to the most eastern of the San Blas Islands and felt sure that sufficient money would buy local marine transport. I intended to retake previous pictures, because since the early eighties slides are now housed in plastic mounts and the edges are no longer frayed. Also in the earlier years I took fewer exposures. Now the level of study had reached the peak of thoroughness and there were places which required more angles of documentation. Through the good offices of the Panamanian Tourist Bureau, I was introduced to René Gómez. René was to help me enjoy the final dimension to following Francis Drake in Panamá.

During the Easter of 1992 I had to enter Colombia to find a recently realised, topographically misunderstood and vaguely located anchorage. This constituted the easternmost end of a route that entailed returning to central Panamá by covering 230 miles in motorised dug-out canoes. This expedition was a successful action-packed adventure. I had reached every anchorage east of the River Chagres. Easter 1993 would enable me to complete the coverage of Drake's movements in western Panamá. This included the remote province of Veragua.

The cost of this expedition had been halved by the presence of retired government scientist, Mr John Thrower, who had read about my work in a national newspaper. This 61 years young Drake scholar had physically conditioned himself to surmount the rigours of this stimulating and rewarding expedition, which he described as an adventure of a lifetime. It was refreshing to learn from, and exchange Drake related information with a man possessing a keen pair of eyes for archaeological detail, coupled with his scientific knowledge.

We returned in 1994 accompanied by 40 year old history teacher, Susan Jackson. Susan had never been abroad and coaxing her to venture into the Panamanian jungle was a slow, persuasive and tender affair. Susan overcame all the challenges to return home elated and, like John, joined the exclusive ranks of the very few who had followed Sir Francis overseas.

There was a most pleasant return visit for a week in January 1996. I was co-presenting a BBC Drake TV documentary marking the 400th anniversary of Drake's death. I then flew to Ecuador to replace the 1981 land view of Cape San Francisco with pictures taken from a boat.

APPENDIX II

The Nombre De Dios That Drake Knew
John Thrower

Introduction

Nombre de Dios is a name that immediately brings 16th century history to mind. The city and its surrounds were very important locations in Francis Drake's career. In 1573, within three miles of Nombre de Dios, Drake established his fortune, which made possible all else that followed. Also between Nombre de Dios and Portobelo he died at sea in 1596 - an ironical twist of fate.

Drake sailed out of Plymouth Sound on 24 May 1572 on a voyage to Tierra Firme - that included today's Panama, for which he had very carefully prepared. He made his objective very clear, *with intent to land at Nombre de Dios.* On his last voyage in 1595/6, the final objective was the City of Panama but the key location was once again Nombre de Dios, from where his troops attempted the land crossing of the isthmus. When that failed, Drake put Nombre de Dios to the torch.

The Nombre de Dios that Drake knew in 1572, was a fair sized city for those days. The settlement had been granted its status by Emperor Charles V in 1537 and had seen some fifty years of development. It was the important terminal for the Tierra Firme treasure fleet, which had, by 1564, established a regular annual timetable. Here it met the treasure mule-trains which had crossed via the Camino Real from Panama City.

The Nombre de Dios that Drake knew in 1596 was at zenith of its development and had exported enormous wealth during the century, including about 200,000 tons of silver. However its harbour suffered several disadvantages. Consequently in 1587 Baptista Antonelli, Philip II's engineer and surveyor, recommended relocation to Portobelo. However, the merchants were reluctant to relocate. Even after Drake sacked the city, they returned! A major fire later in the year, finally convinced them. Moreover relocation took several years to complete. After that Nombre de Dios was abandoned to the jungle. In 1684 William Dampier commented, *Nombre de Dios, a city once famous, is now nothing but a name. For I have lain ashore in the place where that City stood but it is all overgrown with wood, so as to leave no sign that any Town hath been there.*

The Nombre de Dios that Drake knew is a lost city - it no longer exists.

Nombre de Dios Today, The Need For Renewed Investigation

For over 200 years after the city was abandoned the area around the famous bay remained unpopulated. When settlers did return, the new community grew up to the east, leaving the colonial site untouched. This becomes clear today, when one travels to Nombre de Dios by road from Portobelo. After crossing the wide Nombre de Dios river by the new iron girder bridge the road turns to a straight north-east along the former airstrip with low ground and palm plantations on each side. Ahead the blue waters of Nombre de Dios Bay may be glimpsed. Turning east at the bay and passing the cemetery the road divides on the outskirts of the modern village. Here there is a sign announcing Nombre de Dios with a faded and defaced account of its history. However one is quite unaware that the site of the colonial city has already been crossed and passed by. In marked contrast to the well preserved ruins of Panama La Vieja (Old Panama) and of Portobelo, Old Nombre de Dios lies unnoticed, unmarked and un-mapped. It is completely neglected and in danger of destruction.

Parts of the site were rediscovered in 1976 by Dean Edwin Webster. Some remains of the old city had been revealed by clearances for agriculture, which fortunately were by superficial and non-invasive methods. An outline of the old city was visible and stones of a principal street were seen. There was a limited investigation by collection of surface finds and also plans for excavation and survey work under Spanish sponsorship, which unfortunately came to nothing. Although the position of the site was described broadly in relation to the remaining 16th century landmarks, the fort and the Morro (hill or headland) were not mapped. The presence of the old remains and their potential for valuable archaeology seems to have been quickly forgotten.

When Michael Turner and John Thrower visited Nombre de Dios in 1993, they were vexed to find that there were open-cast manganese mining operations nearby and apparently, impinging on to the site. It was quite easy to pick up 16th century artefacts at the southern end of the mined area. Hence it was feared that all the colonial remains might in time be destroyed. The effort was made to inform the responsible authority, the Department of Patrimonio Historico at the National Museum in Panama City, of the dangers. They were unaware of this activity and in no position to take any protective action. The mining operations have now ceased, so the opportunity was taken on a further visit of three days to Nombre de Dios in April 1999 to examine and survey the remaining 16th century landmarks, so as to position them on a modern map by GPS for the first time! By this means and by various land measurements the possible 16th century coastline and the site of the colonial city can also be referred on to the same map. Present day surface features now over the old city site can be described and the remaining potential for archaeology assessed.

This new work is particularly important for the Drake historian. Close reference to the 16th century maps and documents, allied to the results of survey, allows a better assessment of the large physical changes which have taken place at Nombre de Dios Bay during the last 400 years or more. From this a more precise reconstruction of the size and position of the old city, its defences and surrounding trails becomes possible. Drake's challenges, particularly during his attack in 1572, become clearer and his movements can be assessed and discussed in more detail.

16th Century Maps And Documents

From the point of view of the present study, items from the 16th century record which, pointed to the size, layout, facilities and position of the old city were of prime interest. Surprisingly, only three maps remain, which are: the 1541 Vaca de Castro map; a 1570s colour drawing from *The Drake Manuscript*; and the *Paris Profile* from Drake's last voyage. There are four useful descriptions: *Francis Drake Revived* 1572/3; Baptista Antonelli 1587; *The Last Voyage of Drake and Hawkins,* 1596 and the account of the fire in Nombre de Dios in 1596. Add to these various other facts culled from the primary Spanish

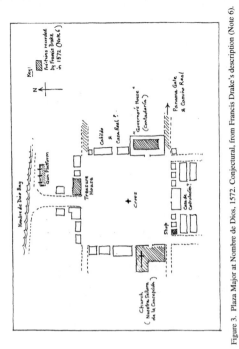

Figure 3. Plaza Major at Nombre de Dios, 1572. Conjectural, from Francis Drake's description (Note 6).

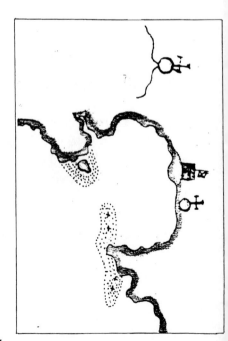

Figure 2. Nombre de Dios, by Licenciado Vaca de Castro (Note 3).

Figure 1. Nombre de Dios Bay, 1541, by Licenciado Vaca de Castro (Note 3).

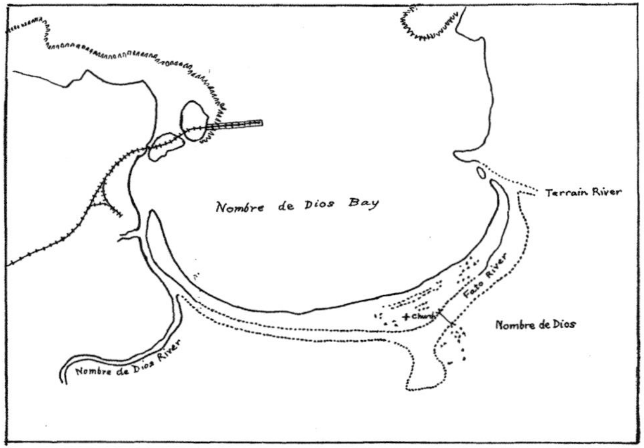

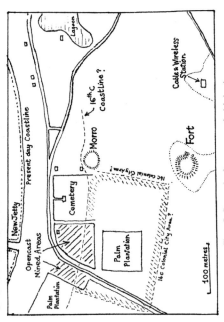

Figure 7. Present day features over colonial city site.

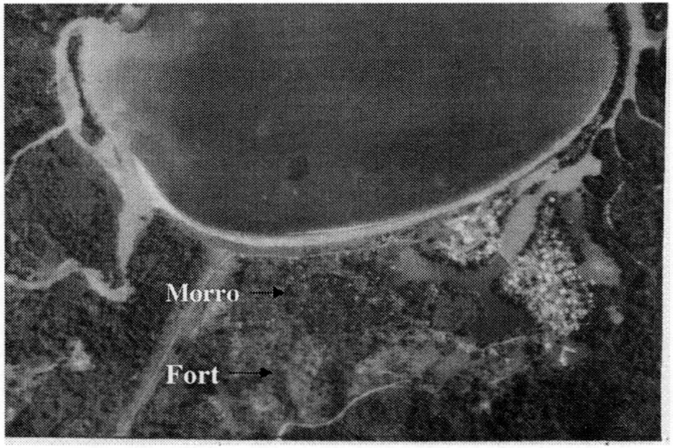

Figure 8. Elevations in metres, colonial city site.

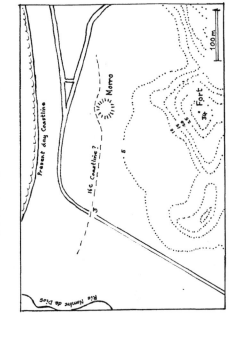

Figure 5. Nombre de Dios Bay, 1914. Survey by U.S.S. Hannibal (Note 15).

Figure 6. Nombre de Dios Bay, 1981. Aerial survey showing fort and Morro.

245

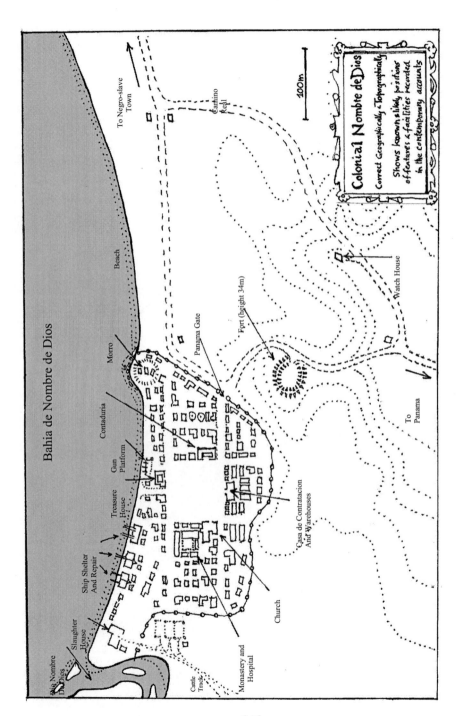

Bahia de Nombre de Dios

Rio Nombre
De Dios

Slaughter
House

Ship Shelter
And Repair

Treasure
House

Gun
Platform

Contaduria

Morro

Beach

To Negro-slave
Town

Camino
Real

Panama Gate

Fort (height 34m)

Watch House

Casa de Contratacion
And Warehouses

Church

Monastery and
Hospital

Cattle
Track

To
Panama

Colonial Nombre de Dios

Correct Geographically & Topographically

Shows known sited positions
of features & facilities recorded
in the contemporary accounts

100m

246

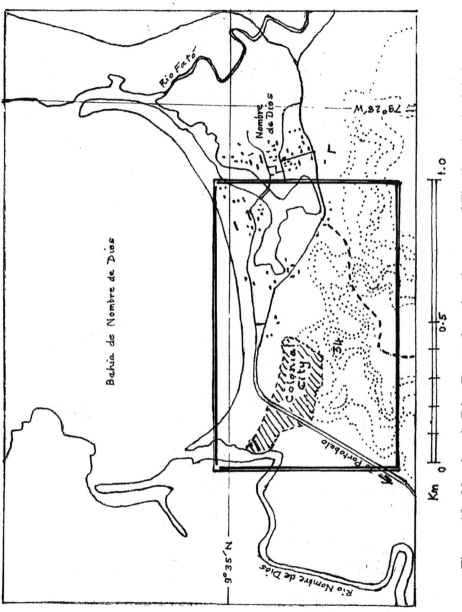

Figure 10. Nombre de Dios Bay today, showing area of Fig. 9 and colonial site.

sources, and the whole interacts and combines to provide considerable detail.

The old maps, in the style of the time, are as much drawings of the city and bay. Both the 1541 (Fig.1) and Drake Manuscript representations show the rocky Morro at the east end of the city, on the tidal edge, with the stones at the base actually projecting into the sea. Originally the Morro was to be the site of the fort. The 1541 drawing also shows the hill to the south, where the fort was actually built. Interestingly the 1541 drawing shows not only a river at the east end (Rio Fató) but also two river exits into the western end of the bay. Perhaps this represents two branches of the Nombre de Dios river through its delta. The city is shown extending from the Morro in the east to the river in the west. The Camino Real is clearly marked leaving the south-east corner of the city and passing between the Morro and the fort. The Drake manuscript depicts the buildings, a few of which were to the east of the Morro, mostly had tiled roofs. It also shows the Camino Real descending from the hills behind the town. The River Nombre de Dios appears at the north-west corner of the bay.

The Paris Profile (Fig. 2) is less detailed of the town, since it includes a stretch of coastline either side of the bay. For visual convenience it is enlarged and orientated to show north at the top. The shape of the bay compares well with modern maps. The fort is shown clearly to the east of the city, which is represented by the church.

Perhaps unnoticed before is the marked projection of the land into the sea directly north of the fort. In such a careful drawing it can hardly be seen as a slip of the map- maker's pen. It must indeed represent the Morro, once again confirming its position.

Baptista Antonelli's meagre description of Nombre de Dios as a city of just thirty households with a seasonal population has gained a firm foothold in the literature. However, as a engineer and surveyor, he had a vested interest. He "wrote down" Nombre de Dios as much as possible in order to persuade a parsimonious King to move the treasure port around the coast to Portobelo. His ploy is revealed, when he comes to extol the advantages of the new harbour. Here we learn about the ease of transport of the many important buildings at Nombre de Dios to the new location. His list of timber buildings with tiled roofs includes at least sixty houses, the church, a casa de contratación (house of trade) and merchants' warehouses. Another Spanish report states that there were 200 houses.

English reports present quite a different dimension: a fair sized city for those days, with a number of facilities. A considerable list collected from the various sources includes: the plaza mayor; (the main square) a main street leading up to the square from the beach; other large streets leading into it with tall buildings; the Panama gate leading to the Camino Real; government buildings; the main church with its associated buildings; the treasure house; shops; warehouses; the slaughterhouse; a watch-house; a mill above the city; the fort on the east side; gun platform; ship shelters and repair facilities on the beach; Negro settlement to the east with another church.

Although no plans exist for the colonial city, Francis Drake's account of his temporary occupation, on 29 July 1572, is sufficiently detailed to allow locations to be assigned to some major buildings and to permit reasonable speculation about the position of others.

(Fig. 3) His descriptions agree within the bounds of the contemporary Spanish reports.

Drake conducted a pitched battle across the main square with the defending Spaniards drawn up on the south side. The impression is given of a large square. Plentiful space would have been needed to accommodate pack trains of up to 200 mules for unloading and loading. Also in addition to their shops, merchants erected tents and booths there when the Tierra Firme Fleet was in harbour. Thus, the square was probably as large and may even have exceeded that at the City of Panama - about 75m x 75m. There was a cross and tree at its centre. A large building with a walled courtyard was identified by Drake as the Governor's house. From the description the complex must have included the contaduria (counting house), where treasure was recorded before being shipped. This building needed to be capable of storing massive loads of bullion and could have approached the size of the corresponding structure built at Portobelo in 1630, which in the 1990s, was restored with a grant from Spain.

Possibly also on the east side would be a casa real, accommodation for the royal officials, known to be in the city from time to time. A cabildo (city hall) probably also fronted the square on the same side. Here were the offices of the city council of Nombre de Dios, much of whose correspondence survives in the archives at Seville. The stone built treasure house stored gold and other high value items. It stood *near the seaside*. It was possible to go around behind it to gain access to the street from the east without entering the square. Its counterpart still stands at Portobelo.

On the western side, to the south, was the Church of Nuestra Señora de La Concepción, known to be large and spacious. Other religious buildings on this side might have included the Dominican Monastery. There was a considerable body of ecclesiastics known to be resident in the city. Possibly the hospital mentioned in a description of 1575 and also referred to in the account of the 1596 fire might also have been nearby but more towards the seashore for health reasons.

The fort on the east side of the city had not been equipped with ordnance in 1572. However, three or four pieces were installed by 1596, one of which ruptured when fired at the English fleet. The city often garrisoned troops: 100 - 150 were recorded in 1572 and a similar number kept the fort during the English attack in 1596.

The shops mentioned by the English would most likely have been on the south side of the square. There is a definite mention of one shop in this position in one of the Spanish reports of 1572. Possibly the casa de contratación was also in this area as indicated by Vaca de Castro. Maybe the associated warehouses were behind the shops to the south. The English reported that there was still a show of merchandise in these shops in 1596 but the warehouses had been cleared. Although the English burnt the city, it recovered remarkably quickly. Perhaps the destruction was less than had been described. At least eighteen businesses had been re-established in a few months and many residents had returned. About sixty of their names appear in the account of the fire. For example Juan Gómez, a carpenter, had his house and business next to, or facing, the Morro. Large quantities of merchandise and ship's stores had been moved back into the city, much of it to be destroyed. The total of the parts of it that were valued came to 750,000 pesos.

The above information enables us to draw some definite conclusions about the size and population of the city. Details are sparse but enough can be assembled to suggest an important and sizeable terminal for the export and import business across the isthmus, either over the Camino Real or via the River Chagres and the Cruces trail. Some major requirements, which, obviously, must have been present there, have not gained a mention in the records; not least, stabling for about 500 mules, comparable with the large facility at the City of Panama. One safe conclusion is that the royal surveyor Antonelli's description is so partial as to be ridiculous.

In 1596, the English described the city as *bigge*. Francis Drake's claim, relating to 1572, that Nombre de Dios was *at least as big as Plymouth* has often been dismissed as braggadocio. It has to be remembered that the early 16th century built up area of Plymouth occupied only about 300 x 400 yards and that its population did not reach 2,000 until the end of the century. At Nombre de Dios both southern corners of the large bay were populated: those of Spanish descent in the west were exceeded in number by the slaves living at the east end of the bay at Santiago del Principe. Many of the slaves would work in the main city during the day. When the Tierra Firme fleet was in harbour, the total population would have exceeded that of Plymouth by a good margin. Much permanent infrastructure to cope with that influx clearly had to be, and was, present.

After the city was abandoned, the name remained. Some of the 18th century maps mark the "ruins of Nombre de Dios" but modern maps carry no indication of the old city. The best modern map is that by the U.S. Defence Mapping agency (DMA) based on the 1981 aerial survey. It does not of course show the new roads constructed in 1984. Some errors have been found, caused by mis-identification of features from aerial photographs. At present it is still a reliable guide to the shape of the beach and sandbars around the bay. It also shows very well the form of the higher ground just to the south of the bay. Figure 4 shows the area around the bay redrawn from the DMA map.

It is interesting to compare the DMA map with the survey made by U.S.S. Hannibal in 1914. Figure 5 shows the corresponding area, again, redrawn from the original. The way that the River Nombre de Dios flows into the bay has changed considerably during the sixty-seven years between the two maps. The most striking change, however, is the revelation that the two main deltas were completely linked by an inland lagoon in 1914.

It is no surprise that none of the 16th century maps shows any indication of deposited sand bars in the bay. These would either have been much smaller features or be hidden under water at that time. However, both modern maps seem to indicate that the River Nombre de Dios may, at times, have had two exits into the western side of the bay, as shown by Vaca de Castro.

The Remaining 16th Century Landmarks

The Camino Real (trail) is located to the south of the modern village (Fig. 4). The track is deeply indented into the hillside next to the highest prominence behind the bay. With commanding views this was undoubtedly the site of the 16th century watch- house. In 1596, the English pursuing the fleeing

Spanish up the trail found *20 sowes of silver, two bars of gold,"* and other valuables here. In 1993/4, although there was a navigational beacon in place, the general ambience of the 16th century was preserved. In 1999 all was changed. Two concrete wheel ways had been laid over the old trail to the top. On the site of the old watch house there is now the building of a Cable & Wireless station with a tall mast surrounded by a high fence and locked gates. GPS readings were taken at the top of the hill to check the position of the trail on the map. Fortunately the rest of the trail is unaltered and remains in daily use. It may be followed for three miles, through the hills, across a plain, where Francis Drake ambushed the mule train on 29 April 1573 and then enters the River Nombre de Dios.

The fort is on a grass and tree covered eminence, which affords another good view of the bay. The shape of the 16th century earthworks is still clearly visible. A graded path leads up and around the north face to reach an entrance on the east side. The remains of the ramparts show around the top, which is flat, roughly circular and about forty metres across. In 1976 portions of the broken cannon, fired at the English in 1596, were discovered. Although the fort can be fairly readily found by walking in its general direction through a good deal of undergrowth, it was difficult in the circumstances of brief visits in 1993 and 1994 to realise its position. It is not marked on any modern map. In 1999 GPS readings revealed that it occupied the hill marked 34m on the DMA map (Fig. 4) Familiarity with its position enabled the fort to be recognised on the aerial photograph (Fig. 6)

The Morro can be reached by a path from the southern road of Nombre de Dios. It is a large rocky knoll about 5m higher than its present surroundings. In 1993 and 1994 it was surrounded by trees with some growing on its sides. The flat top was grass-covered with some exposed rock and occupied by a farm house and livestock. The breech end of the broken cannon, found on the fort, was also here.

In 1999 all was changed. The major part of the Morro had been reduced to ground level. Its stone had been removed and used to convert the temporary pontoon jetty of the mining company into a permanent structure. It seemed a pity that a landmark, which had survived so long, should be sacrificed for a somewhat dubious purpose. Fortunately the northern quarter remained complete with the face which had projected into the sea in Drake's day. Formerly, the Morro may have been about thirty metres across at its base. GPS measurement at the centre of the base on the north face gave $9^0 34.895'$ N, $79^0 28.436'$ W. The original position of the Morro in relation to its surroundings was now somewhat easier to assess because so much vegetation had been cleared. The former centre was due east and opposite to the southern end of the east wall of the cemetery. Knowledge of its position meant that the Morro could be recognised on the aerial photograph (Fig. 6)

The 16th Century Coastline And The Colonial Site Today

The north face of the Morro is approximately 130m to the south of the present-day coastline. Allowing for the projection of the Morro into the sea, a possible "16th century coastline" is shown on the larger scale map (Fig. 7), following the curve of the bay, for few hundred metres to the west. The approximation is reasonable taking into account that the shape of the bay is similar on all old and modern maps.

To the north of the Morro and to the south of the road which follows the line of the beach, the land is relatively low lying. It continues in this way to the west but more especially to the east towards the present lagoon, which divides the modern village. Parts of the area are inclined to flood in the rainy season. The roads are built up but between them some shanties are built on stilts. Clearly, the area corresponds to the continuous lagoon recorded on the 1914 map. The southern extent of that lagoon in the old city area must have been close to the 16th century coastline.

The old city was built close to its seashore. In 1572 Francis Drake observed that he stepped onto a beach, *not past twenty yards from the houses*. Antonelli noted in 1587 that the city was, *builded on a sandy bay, hard by the seaside*. Therefore to see what present-day features lie over the site, the area of interest is a rectangle behind the old coastline towards the river, certainly across the road to Portobelo and south from the Morro to the base of the fort.
(Fig. 7)

The first feature to the west of the Morro is the cemetery, enclosed by a wall. The east and west walls had originally been built into the undergrowth. There is no south wall. The position of the cemetery was confirmed by land and GPS measurements and by comparison with the aerial photograph (Fig. 6) In 1999 only about 60% of the cemetery was in use. The remaining and southerly 40% was overgrown jungle. Adjacent and outside the west wall was a three metre wide path running due south from the road.

Next, to the west, is the main area subjected to open cast mining between the cemetery and the road and a smaller mined area to the west of the road. Mining has ceased but the area has not been restored; spoil heaps and rusting machinery remain and work on the jetty is incomplete. The mined areas extend southwards to the same extent as the cemetery walls. The 1981 aerial photograph shows that these areas were already cleared then and were undoubtedly associated with the airstrip constructed in 1959. The small building near the road was the ticket office.

Figure 7 depicts that the cemetery and mined areas are crossed by the old coastline at an angle. Thus about three-quarters of the cemetery and perhaps two-thirds of the mined areas were then under the sea. Correspondingly and bearing in mind that there was a twenty metre beach, there has not been much incursion onto the old city site by these modern developments. Since the southern portion of the cemetery remained undeveloped during our visit, the most damage is at the southern end of the mined areas.

A large part of the area of interest is on a level with the rear of the cemetery (Fig. 8). There was abundant space here for the city square and surrounding buildings. Towards the south-east the ground rises steadily, gently at first and then steeply towards the fort. Any parts of the old city, which were built here, would have enjoyed views of the bay and pleasant sea breezes. Much of this land was cleared of forest for agriculture in 1976; some is still relatively clear and several homesteads are established. The remainder is lightly tree covered with one area of dense and fenced palm plantation. To the west of the road and across to the river is another large fenced palm plantation, where we unearthed some late 16th century crockery. From the path by the cemetery one may take a pleasant walk through woodlands as the land rises, finally making a steep climb towards the fort.

Colonial Nombre De Dios And Environs

Figure 9 shows a conjectural plan of the old city and a map of its surroundings, accurately scaled for the DMA map. To prepare this the following were considered:

a) The 16th century coastline, determined as already discussed (Fig. 7) correctly positioned and allowing for the projection of the Morro on to the beach as a headland.

b) The fort and Morro accurately positioned and to scale.

c) The form of the high ground to the south drawn and scaled from the DMA map.

d) The watch house in its correct position on the highest prominence behind the bay as discussed (Fig. 7)

e) The internal plan of the city, conjectural, but derived by extension of Figure 3. The Plaza Mayor was about 100 metres square and placed centrally.

f) The external boundaries of the city, also conjectural but take account of the following:

    i)   There were buildings around the Morro as this is the area where the fire started in 1596.

    ii)   From the Morro to the Panama Gate, the boundary follows a south-west direction to allow for the Camino Real (trail) to approach the gate on level ground between the boundary and higher ground, bearing in mind that the slopes up to the fort would be kept clear as lines of fire.

iii) The southern boundary takes account of the form of the higher ground to its south. It might extend more to the south but the need to keep a line of fire clear from the fort must be kept in mind.

iv) The south-west boundaries cut back as shown taking account of soft low ground near the river and the approach of the cattle track from the south.

v) The western extremity of the city towards the river would have needed to take account of some form of entrance from the cattle track and the need to accommodate the slaughter house on the beach near the river.

g) The trails:

i) Up to the fort from the Panama Gate - part of this trail still exists.

ii) Across the saddle from the fort to the higher ground to the south. This trail exists as a path. It would have joined the Camino Real at the top, south of the watch house as shown.

iii) From the south the main Camino Real would pass the branch-off to the fort and, after passing the watch house, descend the more gentle slope to the north-east, finally reaching level ground. It would

iii) then branch to the west to reach the city and to the east to the Negro-slave town.

Conclusions

It has been established that there is still some scope for valuable archaeology at the colonial site - abandoned to the jungle at the turn of the 16th century. The site remains largely untouched - a unique opportunity. Of course, there is not now the same ideal chance for immediate investigation that Edwin Webster identified in 1976. However much of the site remains undeveloped and some parts are relatively clear, especially to the south of the cemetery. A team equipped with modern geophysical equipment could survey the site quickly to determine its remaining potential.

This study has provided the historian with a much clearer picture of the object of Francis Drake's attacks in 1572 and 1596. We now have better background information to interpret and to discuss the contemporary records in more detail.

Main Sources And Selected Bibliography

| C. L. G. Anderson | *Old Panama & Castilla Del Oro* | Boston, 1911 |

| William Dampier | *A New Voyage Around The World,* Argonaut Edition | London, 1927 |

| Crispin Gill | *Plymouth, A New History* | Devon, 1993 |

| Richard Hakluyt | *Principal Navigations,* Everyman edition, Vol. 7 | London, 1907 |

| William H. Prescott | *The History Of The Conquest of Peru,* Routledge Edition, Vol. 3, | Boston 1847 |

John Thrower	*The Lost Treasure of Sir Francis Drake*	Dorset, 1996
John Thrower	*Colonial Nombre de Dios*	Dorset, 2000
Michael Turner	*In Drakes' Wake*	unpublished
Edwin C. Webster,	*Nombre de Dios*	Panamá, 1977

Histoire Naturelle Des Indies - The Drake Manuscript,
New York, 1996

Manuscripts Anglaise, 51 Folio 13, Bibliotheque Nationale, Paris

Sir Francis Drake Revived, London, 1626

The Fire At Nombre de Dios 1596, British Library,

Add MS 13977, folios 163-167

Hakluyt Society Series 2, Vol. 71, (1932) and Vol. 142, (1972)

Chronology of Colonial Nombre de Dios

1502		Columbus names Bastimentos Island and Portobelo.
1509	8 March	Nombre de Dios founded by Diego de Nicuesa.
1509		Henry VIII King of England.
1593	25 Sept	Balboa reaches the Pacific Ocean.
1516		Acla founded by Balboa.
1516	15 March	Charles V King of Spain.
1519		Panama City founded.
1520		Shift from Acla to Nombre de Dios. The existing Camino Real widened.
1524		Francisco Pizarro's passed through the city on his first Pacific expedition.
1526		Don Pedro de los Rios, the new governor arrives at Nombre de Dios.
1526-7		Pizarro's second Pacific expedition.
1528		Pizarro embarks for Spain at Nombre de Dios.
1529		Pizarro appointed governor of Peru.
1530		Pizarro returns from Spain to Nombre de Dios, met by Almargo.
1533		From Nombre de Dios, Hernando Pizarro embarks for Spain, with a huge cargo of gold.
1537	29 Nov	Nombre de Dios granted city status by Charles V.
1540		*Francis Drake born.*
1544	Jan	Blasco Nuñez de Vela, Viceroy of Peru arrives at Nombre de Dios.

1545		Silver Mountain discovered at Potosí, Bolivia.
1546		Pedro de la Gasca Viceroy of Peru arrives at Nombre de Dios.
1553		Mary I Queen of England.
1556		Philip II King of Spain.
1558		Elizabeth I Queen of England.
1564		Convoy system between the New World and Spain fully developed.
1572	29 July	Francis Drake attacks Nombre de Dios.
1573	29 April	Francis Drake captures the mule train 2.5 miles south of the city.
1587		Thomas Cavendish enters the Pacific and causes severe delay to the Plate Fleet at Nombre de Dios.
1587		Baptista Antonelli advises Phillip II to re-route the Camino Real to Portobelo.
1595		Sir Richard Hawkins' men embark for Spain from Nombre de Dios.
1595-6		Sir Francis Drake occupies the city whilst Baskerville is repulsed at Capirilla Pass.
1596	13 Aug	Disastrous fire at the reoccupied Nombre de Dios.
1597-1601		Nombre de Dios gradually abandoned in favour of Portobelo.
1598		Death of Philip II.
1603		Death of Elizabeth I.

APPENDIX III

Francis Drake's Treasure Haul 29 April 1573
John Thrower

When fifteen English led by Francis Drake and twenty French led by Guillaume Le Testu successfully ambushed a 190 mule-train near Nombre de Dios, they must have been truly amazed to see such a massive amount of gold and silver bullion: riches beyond their wildest dreams. They carefully collected all the gold which was in various forms of bars, quoits (heavy discs) and coined metal. Most of the gold would have been of 22 carat purity. Unable to deal with the enormous weight of silver, they buried as much of this they could, about fifteen tons, before the return of the Spanish guards with reinforcements from Nombre de Dios.

Some twenty years later, Drake edited the English account of this ambush, which was *"faithfully taken out of the reports of Christopher Ceeley, Ellis Hixon and others"* by Philip Nichols, Preacher. Drake was quite specific about the amount of silver on the mule-train, which he estimated to be about thirty tons, but which he was forced to leave mostly behind. He was curiously reticent, however, about the amount of gold that the raiders had carried off:

"and being weary, we were contented with a few bars and quoits of gold as we could well carry."

This is a definite Drake joke or "leg-pull" at the expense of the reader, of which there are a number in the account! However there is more than a hint here about the problems they faced in carrying off the heavy metals.

Drake's account was finally published, by his nephew, in 1626 as *Sir Francis Drake Revived*. Amazingly, it was not until more than 300 years later, in 1932, following the painstaking work of Irene Wright in translating the carefully stored records in Seville, that the English, Spanish and later the French accounts could be matched and discussed together. Even so most major Drake historians since 1932 have not troubled to evaluate one of the most important points - *the weight of gold that the raiders had secured.* This weight tells us everything about the hard task Drake's and Le Testu's men had to accomplish to return twenty-one miles through coastal jungle to the River Francisco.

The Spanish records allow us to penetrate Drake's reticence - they give a maximum figure of 130,000 pesos for the gold on the mule-train. But what was the weight of all this gold? The peso, in this case the *peso de oro*, was a measure of weight of 22 - carat gold. It was equivalent to one hundreth (0.01) of a Spanish pound weight. In its turn, the Spanish pound weight was slightly heavier than the English pound avoir - 1.014 lb. Thus the 130,000 pesos of gold on the mule-train weighed an astonishing 1,318 lb - *well over half a ton!*

There is another useful method by which one may cross-check on this figure. The Elizabeth I £1 coin was also minted in a known weight of 22 - carat gold, a 0.0249 lb avoir. Since the peso de oro was worth 8s 3d in 1573, a value mentioned in *Sir Francis Drake Revived*, a simple calculation gives 1,337 lb for the 130,000 pesos - a good agreement with the above figure, considering the accuracy of minting in those days.

Over half a ton of gold meant that the English and French were quite sufficiently burdened with gold alone. They could not possibly carry awkward silver bars as well - heavy for their value - though, no doubt, some tried to do so. The silver would have been for the allies, the Cimmarones to carry. We do not know how many Cimmarones were with Drake's party, but even if there were as many as forty, they would have had severe difficulty in carrying away as much as two tons of silver. The gold represented a full load for four mules. So, the remaining 186 mules were carrying 300 pounds of silver each, amounting altogether to 55,800 lb, some twenty-five tons. One can readily understand how it was that the returning Spaniards found so much just lying around.

What was the value of Drake's treasure haul? Of course one can calculate the modern value of the weight of gold - some £3.5 million for 100,000 pesos. However there are several problems here. Most important is that the gold today is much less valuable than it was in the 16th century. Also, the gold price varies significantly from day-to-day and substantially from year-to-year. Although the price has risen sharply in the present period of uncertainty, it has been at a relatively low level in recent years. It is worth less now than it was ten years ago, when I first made some of these calculations! The value of the pure gold in an Elizabethan £1 coin was a measly £86 ten years ago; it has now fallen to £79. This makes a nonsense of an attempt to compare values on this basis and does not even begin to reflect inflation since the 16th century.

Various Drake biographers and other historians have made estimates at different times, each trying to relate Tudor versus modern values at the date of publication. Inevitably these rapidly become dated. A recent example is Alison Weir's book

- Henry VIII, King and Court, she uses a factor of 300 to convert £1 Tudor to modern value in the year 2000. This factor works well for some items but is less suitable for others. 300 is an overall average; some Tudor products were relatively more expensive than today and others cheaper. For example, if one were to employ a factor of 300 to convert the £3,400 that Francis Drake paid to purchase Buckland Abbey, today's price would be £1,020,000 - much too low - a factor of at least 1,000 and probably more would be needed Looking back to Drake's 1573 gold, 130,000 pesos, corresponds to £53,625 Elizabethan. Of course he was obliged to share this with the French, but we know that the English, ultimately had the larger share. The total sum, on its own would have been sufficient to purchase Buckland Abbey sixteen times over! This may sound fantastic, but perhaps gives a better feel for the value of the treasure to Francis Drake. It was the turning point of his career, He gained influence, and it made possible the building of the *Golden Hind*. Clearly there has to be an advance from the overall multiplying factor of 300 discussed above - perhaps to at least 400 which would value the total treasure haul to well over £20 million today.

The factor to convert value will go on increasing into the future. However one thing remains constant, that is the shear weight of very heavy gold, twice as dense as lead, with which the raiders had to struggle over steep hills, across rivers and through jungle, in torrid, sticky heat back to the Rio Francisco.

Weight and Value of Gold and Silver on Mule Train

Gold

Gold weight calculation based on:

1. The weight of the gold peso (peso de oro) 22 carat gold. This is defined as one hundred (0.01) of the Spanish pound = 1.014 lb avoir.

2. The comparative weight of the gold peso to that of the Elizabeth I £1 coin (22 carat) since the peso was worth 8s 3d i.e. 0.4125 £ Elizabeth I.

Gold weight (22 carat) on mule train

1. 100,000 pesos = 1000 x 1.014 = 1,014 lb avoir
   130,000 pesos = 1300 x 1.014 = 1,318 lb avoir

2. £1 Elizabeth I = 174.5 grains 22 carat gold
   Gold peso = 174.5 x 0.4125 = 72 grains 22 carat gold (7,000 grains = 1 lb avoir)

100,000 pesos = 7,200,000 ÷ 7,000 = 1,028 lb avoir
130,000 pesos = 9,360,000 ÷ 7,000 = 1,337 lb avoir (half a ton 1,120 lb)

King's gold recovered by Spaniards

11 gold bars, 6,300 pesos = 65 lb

Modern value of pure gold (round figures)

	Troy oz	Elizabethan pound	Gold peso	100,000 peso
January 1994	£258	£86	£36	£3,600,000
November 2004	£238	£79	£33	£3,300,000

Silver on Mule Train

There were 190 mules; since four were carrying gold, 186 were carrying silver.

186 carrying 300lb silver bars each equals 186 x 300
= 55,800lb or about 25 tons.

Number and size of silver bars.
Take 50lb as an example of the weight of one silver ingot.

Then there were $\frac{55,800}{50}$ = 1,116 bars on the mule train.

Frances Drake buried 15 tons = $\frac{33,600lb}{50}$ = 672 50lb bars.

Volume of a 50lb silver bar = 2,250 cm^3. So, if a bar is 30cm long, then the width is 7.5cm and the depth 10cm, or 1ft x 3in x 4½ in.

Modern value of pure silver (round figures)

	Troy oz	55,800lb
January 1994	£42	£2,343,000
November 2004	£58	£3,236,000